CREATION VERSUS CHAOS

CREATION
VERSUS
CHAOS

The Reinterpretation of
Mythical Symbolism in the Bible

BERNHARD W. ANDERSON

Professor of Biblical Theology
The Theological School
Drew University

ASSOCIATION PRESS

NEW YORK

CREATION VERSUS CHAOS

BT
695
A5

Publisher's stock number: 1632

Library of Congress catalog card number: 67-14578

To

WILL HERBERG

esteemed colleague and friend

Preface

At the beginning of his first volume of published sermons, Harry Emerson Fosdick observed that sermons, unlike the proverbial child, should be heard, not seen. I have similar misgivings about letting these lectures, which were originally designed for particular audiences, be seen in print. In yielding to requests for publication, I have endeavored to retain as much as possible the original spirit and form of the lectures, though I have expanded certain parts and have documented the discussion in footnotes.

The first four lectures constituted the Nils W. Lund Memorial Lectures in Biblical Studies at the North Park College and Theological Seminary in the fall of 1965. I am grateful to President Karl A. Olsson, Dean Donald C. Frisk, and members of their faculty for the friendly welcome and Christian fellowship experienced during my visit. The four lectures were repeated, and the fifth added, at a theological conference held at St. Olaf College during the summer of 1966. Again I record my appreciation to President Sidney A. Rand, to the conference chairman, Dr. Harold H. Ditmanson, and to faculty members and conference participants for the theological stimulus of that occasion.

7

In these lectures I have attempted to bring into focus, at the point of a particular biblical motif, the scholarly discussions which have engaged my interest for a number of years, especially under the influence of Hermann Gunkel's pioneering work, *Schöpfung und Chaos*. The creation-faith of the Bible is explored from the angle of one of its major motifs: the chaos which ever threatens to overwhelm the order of creation and to plunge history into meaningless confusion. I have endeavored to show how the biblical writers appropriated the motif of the conflict between the Creator and the powers of chaos from the religions of the ancient Near East; they radically reinterpreted the motif, however, so that it is now used poetically in the Scriptures to express a dramatic conflict in which man's existence is at stake. In the biblical perspective, it is maintained, man finds who he is and what life really means, not in relation to nature, with its cycles of death and renewal, but in relation to history, where God calls him to a historical task.

Some of my colleagues—Will Herberg, Lawrence Toombs, and Howard Kee—have read the manuscript and have made helpful comments, though they cannot be held responsible for my stubborn refusal to yield ground in areas of controversy or for my failure to remove every vestige of inconsistency. It is my hope that these lectures may have the effect of drawing readers into an area which too often has been the domain of specialists and to stimulate theological interest in a subject which is closer to our lives than we often realize.

—BERNHARD W. ANDERSON
The Theological School
Drew University

Contents

Contents

CHAPTER

1

Creation and History

SPREADING AROUND THE EARTH like the drifting fallout from a mighty nuclear bomb is a profoundly disturbing sense of disorder. Peoples from various nations, races, and cultural settings are beginning to experience an affinity for each other, not because they agree at the level of political or philosophical discourse but because at the depth of their being they share a common anguish in the face of radical uncertainty. This pervasive sense of disorder finds many expressions. Young people have been singing songs that express an eschatological awareness of living on "the eve of destruction." The widely influential philosopher Paul Tillich used to speak to us of "the sense of the abyss." Others, like Berdyaev, have declared that the image of man has been destroyed, thereby opening the soul to "an invasion of chaos." Some liken our situation to the time of the Great Flood when the waters of chaos broke loose from above and below, or to the overthrow of the Cities of the Plain, Sodom and Gomorrah, whose ruins presumably lie buried beneath the Dead Sea, or to the time of confusion when Rome, the proud upholder of world order, was overwhelmed by a flood of barbarian invaders. It is amazing that back in 1921—well before the Second World War, the atomic holocausts of Nagasaki and Hiroshima, and the ominous chain-reaction of events which have shaped our consciousness—the poet W. B. Yeats prophetically anticipated the world crisis in his familiar lines:

> Things fall apart; the centre cannot hold;
> Mere anarchy is loosed upon the world,
> The blood-dimmed tide is loosed, and everywhere
> The ceremony of innocence is drowned;
> The best lack all conviction, while the worst
> Are full of passionate intensity.[1]

A situation similar to ours provided the occasion for the prophet Jeremiah to compose a little poem on the subject "a vision of cosmic destruction" (Jer. 4:23–26). This moving portrayal of threatening chaos is undoubtedly one of the finest pieces in the literature of ancient Israelite prophecy and, for that matter, in world literature as a whole. It seems to have been composed toward the end of Jeremiah's career, around the fateful turn from the seventh to the sixth centuries B.C., when the nation Judah stood on the eve of destruction. In a terrifying vision the prophet portrays the results of a devastating invasion from the North. His poetic eye sees, however, not just the coming of the Foe from the North, but the invasion of chaos itself, as though the earth were returned to its primeval condition of "waste and void"—the *tohu wa-bohu* that prevailed before the creation, according to the Priestly account (Gen. 1:2). Jeremiah's words are almost unbearable:

> I looked on the earth, and lo, it was waste and void;
> and to the heavens, and they had no light.

----

[1] From "The Second Coming." Reprinted with permission of The Macmillan Company from *Collected Poems* (2nd ed., pp. 184 f.) by William Butler Yeats. Copyright 1924 by The Macmillan Company. Renewed 1952 by Bertha Georgie Yeats. See also in this connection the excellent discussion by Amos N. Wilder in *Modern Poetry and the Christian Tradition: A Study of the Relation of Christianity to Culture* [160], especially Chap. IX.

Note: In the footnotes throughout this book a number enclosed in brackets after a citation refers to the numbered Selected Bibliography at the end of the book, where full information on books and articles is given.

I looked on the mountains, and lo, they were quaking,
    and all the hills moved to and fro.
I looked, and lo, there was no man,
    and all the birds of the air had fled.
I looked, and lo, the fruitful land was a desert,
    and all its cities were laid in ruins
    before the Lord, before his fierce anger.
                                    —JEREMIAH 4:23–26

Now, it surely would be wrong to understand Jeremiah's language as a literal prediction that the God who created the world as a cosmos was about to reduce it to its precreation condition. Here the prophet is using the imagery of chaos *metaphorically;* and the effect of this religious language is "to expand the consciousness, the imaginative grasp of the predicament, to its absolute conditions." [2] When we submit to the "imaginative grasp" of the language, this vision of returning chaos speaks to our time with haunting effectiveness. It is worthy of note that contemporary poets give expression to a similar sense of catastrophe, if not world judgment, and thereby help us to understand dimensions of historical existence to which the Bible bears witness. As Amos Wilder points out, poets like John Masefield and Alfred Noyes, Vachel Lindsay and Edwin Markham, even Robert Browning and Alfred Tennyson, and many others who reflected the buoyant optimism of the nineteenth century doctrine of progress, no longer speak to our situation. Where are the Browning clubs or the Tennyson circles? "Is it any wonder," he asks, "that we go back rather to Herman Melville and his white whale, to Hawthorne and his symbolism of evil, to Blake, to the French symbolists, Rimbaud, Baudelaire, to John Donne, and indeed, to Dante, to Ezekiel, to the Flood, the Fall of Man, and to the original myths of creation and chaos?" [3]

Let me pick up that concluding reference to our going back

---

[2] Stanley R. Hopper, exposition of Jer. 4:23–26 in *The Interpreter's Bible,* [2] Vol. V, pp. 839–42.

[3] A. N. Wilder [160], p. 211. See also S. Hopper, *loc. cit.,* who discusses this observation in his exposition.

to the myths of the Flood, the Fall, and the ancient myths of creation and chaos. One of the conspicuous features of the intellectual climate of the mid-twentieth century is the renewed interest in the myths and sagas of the ancient world. This is evident in modern works of literature, like T. S. Eliot's *The Waste Land* or the *Cantos* of Ezra Pound. It is also manifest in the area of the phenomonology of religion, where fruitful work has been done by such men as G. van der Leeuw, Mircea Eliade, and Paul Ricoeur. These studies are interested in religious phenomena of all men and all times, unbiased by the value judgments usually expressed in the adjectival comparisons between "primitive and modern," "prescientific and scientific," or "pagan and Jewish-Christian." Increasingly it is recognized that one great obstacle in the way of drawing upon the full wealth of human wisdom is the fond idea of evolution, which has been transposed into "cultural progress" or "historical development." Why should it be supposed that men in the twentieth century have any fundamental advantage over previous ages just because men lately have refined the capacity for abstract thought and scientific technology? Why should it be assumed that "historical development" has escalated modern men to a height from which we can look down upon those who preceded us? Once we surrender the proud notion that people in the twentieth century, and especially people whose roots are in the West, are better off than the generations that have gone before, the door is opened for a poetic and philosophic sharing of the riches of human creativity from the dawn of history to the present. Indeed, when modern men are emancipated from contemporaneity, they may discover dimensions of existence shared with all men and all times. The representative poets and artists of today, Wilder remarks, are not concerned primarily with immediate social problems, or recent traditions from a particular land or people, but "with man in his long past and with the ancient sagas and myths, rituals and arts, tumuli and cities, that document his universal story." And, surprising as it may seem, the ancient myths speak to us.

The oldest myths, whether of the Fisher King or of the Fall, whether of Ulysses or of the Tower of Babel, are contemporary. Pattern is given to the welter and jungle of human society not by historical development but by myth. The locus of the soul is not in London or New York or Vienna but at the barred gate of Eden or with Odysseus on his journey, or with Kafka's hero before the court of the unaccountable judges.[4]

I

This brings me to the theme of this study: "Creation Versus Chaos." The formulation of the theme is reminiscent of a book by Hermann Gunkel which appeared many years ago, in 1895: *Schöpfung und Chaos in Urzeit und Endzeit* ("Creation and Chaos in Beginning-time and End-time"). This epoch-making book was one of the most important works of the great pioneer of form-criticism and tradition-history whose influence, somewhat belatedly, has profoundly shaped biblical studies in our time. Throughout the course of our study we shall be dealing repeatedly with Gunkel's contribution.

A couple of decades before Gunkel wrote this pioneering work, the world was electrified by the announcement that Assyrian copies of the Old Babylonian creation and flood stories had been found at Nineveh in the library of Ashurbanipal (669–633 b.c.), the last great king of the Assyrian empire. During his glorious reign Ashurbanipal developed the interests that were stimulated by the excellent education he received in his youth. First of all, he was well trained in warfare and manly sports. These interests were magnificently illustrated in the elaborate reliefs that decorated the walls of his palace in Nineveh: pictures of his hard-hitting warfare against camel-riding Arabs, scenes of his victories against Elam, vivid portrayals of his lion hunts which pulse with the excitement of the chase. In addition, his education included learning to read and write cuneiform, solving mathematical problems, and delving into the wisdom of the sages. These literary and philosophical

---

4 Wilder [160], pp. 206, 212.

interests prompted him to establish a great library in his capital. The Assyrian king sent his scribes throughout Mesopotamia to make careful copies of original documents. In this way tens of thousands of clay tablets were collected in Nineveh. There had been libraries before that time, but Ashurbanipal's library, which attempted to include all Babylonian literature, was a remarkable achievement for its day. Then came the eve of destruction. In 612 b.c., just a few years after Ashurbanipal's death, Nineveh was destroyed under the combined assault of Babylonians, Medes, and Scythians. Nineveh, like Tyre, became an example to the world of imperial glory that had departed. By the time of the Greek historian Xenophon (430–after 355 b.c.) the city was an abandoned ruin. And for almost twenty-five hundred years it remained a dismal memory, its major mound (Tell Kuyunjik) a ruin and a waste, as it is to this very day.

In the middle of the nineteenth century, however, this mound—directly across the Tigris from modern Mosul in Iraq—became the scene of one of the first major excavations in the history of archaeology. The work began under the French in 1842 and continued intermittently under British supervision until 1932. It was well over a century ago (1853) that Hormuzd Rassam, who was at Kuyunjik continuing the excavation led by the Englishman Austin Henry Layard, discovered the palace of Ashurbanipal and the thousands of clay tablets in the library. Rassam shipped the Kuyunjik tablets to the British Museum for decipherment and identification, but it was not until almost twenty years later (1872) that the full significance of the discovery was understood. At that time George Smith, a young Assyriologist employed as an assistant in the British Museum, was sorting and classifying the tablets from Nineveh, when suddenly his eye was arrested by a familiar reference. "Commencing a steady search among these fragments," he wrote later, "I soon found half of a curious tablet which had evidently contained originally six columns. . . . On looking down the third column, my eye caught the statement that the ship rested on the mountains of Nizir, followed by the account of the sending forth of the dove, and its finding no resting-place and returning. I saw at once that I had here discovered a portion at least of the Chaldean account of the Deluge." [5]

But that was not all. Included among the religious texts of this library was the Babylonian myth known as *Enuma elish* after its opening words ("When on high . . .")—a relatively late version of an ancient myth which dates back to at least the First Babylonian Dynasty (ca. 1830–1530 B.C.), whose greatest king was Hammurabi (ca. 1728–1686 B.C.). This myth, first published by George Smith in 1876 under the title *The Babylonian Account of Genesis,* deals with the fateful drama which, according to Mesopotamian belief, occurred in the beginning and was reenacted annually as the old year died out and the new year was born: the struggle between order and chaos represented in the victory of the creator-god Marduk over the powers of disorder and death.[6] The myth was solemnly recited in the temple of Marduk on the fourth day of the Babylonian New Year festival, the *akitu.* And since it deals with a conflict within nature which had existential relevance for ancient man, it is no exaggeration to say, with E. A. Speiser, that it was "the most significant expression of the religious literature of Mesopotamia." [7]

The myth begins with a portrayal of primeval, watery chaos (cf. Gen. 1:2) consisting of the male and female precreation powers: the primordial father, Apsu (fresh-water lakes, marshes,

---

[5] Quoted in Jack Finegan, *Light from the Ancient Past* [49], p. 217.

[6] In an early version of the myth the victor was another deity—according to Thorkild Jacobsen the West Semitic god of lightning and thunderstorm, Baal. The place of this storm god was taken by Marduk, the patron deity of the city of Babylon—a development which presumably reflects the period of the First Babylonian Dynasty when Hammurabi unified Babylonia. See further S. N. Kramer, *Mythologies of the Ancient World* [90], pp. 93–137, who emphasizes the Sumerian background of Akkadian mythology.

[7] *Ancient Near Eastern Texts* [5], p. 60. The myth is also treated by Alexander Heidel, *The Babylonian Genesis* [73]; T. Jacobsen in *The Intellectual Adventure of Ancient Man* [52], pp. 125 ff.; S. G. F. Brandon, *Creation Legends of the Ancient Near East* [20], Chap. III; T. H. Gaster, *The Oldest Stories in the World* [57], pp. 52–70.

and subsoil waters)—from which incidentally our English word *abyss* has come [8]—and the primordial mother, Tiamat (the salty marine waters). Associated with these two seas at the beginning was another power, Mummu, who was also regarded as an aspect of the primeval water.

> When on high the heavens had not been named,
> Firm ground below had not been called by name,
> Naught but primordial Apsu, their begetter,
> (And) Mummu-Tiamat,[9] she who bore them all,
> Their waters commingling as a single body;
> No reed hut had been matted, no marsh land had appeared,
> When no gods whatever had been brought into being,
> Uncalled by name, their destinies undetermined—
> Then it was that the gods were formed within them.[10]

As the final line indicates, the gods were born as a result of the commingling of the male and female waters. In other words, the first act of the creation-drama—even before the origin of the world and man—was "the coming-to-be of the divine," out of anterior chaos.[11] However, the birth of the gods was the occasion for conflict, for the new beings were characterized by activity, while the old water powers represented inertia. In the myth the younger generations of the gods are described as dis-

---

[8] J. V. Kinnier Wilson, in his translation of this creation epic in *Documents from Old Testament Times* [7], observes that Apsu comes from Sumerian *Abzu* which contains as its first element *ab*, "sea," and that the same word reappears in Greek as *abussos*, for instance, the abyss or "bottomless pit" of Rev. 9:1 f., 11.

[9] E. A. Speiser maintains that Mummu here does not refer to the primordial vizier but is perhaps an epithet for "mother." Alternatively, J. V. K. Wilson translates this line: "Only Mummu, and Tiamat who brought all of them forth." So also Jacobsen, who points out that Mummu, Apsu's "page-boy," signifies the primeval liquid form of everything.

[10] Speiser's translation, *Ancient Near Eastern Texts* [5], pp. 60 ff., which will be followed here. The myth is reproduced in shorter form in *The Ancient Near East: An Anthology of Texts and Pictures* [6], pp. 31–39; also *Documents from Old Testament Times* [7], pp. 3–16.

[11] This myth, which deals with "the origin and the end of evil," is discussed incisively by Paul Ricoeur in *The Symbolism of Evil* [132]. We shall return to the bearing of the myth upon the problem of evil especially in Chap. 5.

turbing the peace of their primordial parents: ". . . they trou-
bled the mood of Tiamat by their hilarity"; "Apsu could not
lessen their clamor." So Apsu, who was getting "no rest by day,
by night no sleep," determined to destroy the whole brood of
the gods, a devilish plan in which he was supported by his
vizier, Mummu, against Tiamat, who urged patience. However, the god Ea was able to meet the first threat of the powers
of chaos. Causing a deep sleep to fall over Apsu by means of
a magical incantation, he murdered Apsu in his sleep and
bound Mummu. Ea then rested in his chamber where he and
his wife conceived Marduk, "most potent and wisest of gods."

But the powers of chaos had not yet been overcome. To
avenge herself for the murder of her husband, Tiamat organized an army of rebel gods and fiendish monsters, placing her
second husband, Kingu, at the head as commander in chief.
This formidable host advanced against the gods, bent upon
total destruction. Marduk's father, Ea, who had been victorious against Apsu, declined to make a stand; and the sky-god,
Anu, though bravely going out to meet Tiamat, had to turn
back. The plight of the gods was desperate. Anshar, the chief
of the gods, stared at the ground and the other gods were so
cowed that they sat in silence, "their lips closed tight." In the
crisis Anshar turned to the young god Marduk, asking him to
be the champion of the gods. Marduk consented on the condition that, in spite of his youth, he be given the highest position of authority in the divine assembly.

> If I indeed, as your avenger,
> Am to vanquish Tiamat and save your lives,
> Set up the Assembly, proclaim supreme my destiny!
> When jointly in Ubshukinna [the Assembly Hall] you
>   have sat down rejoicing,
> Let my word, instead of you, determine the fates.
> Unalterable shall be what I may bring into being;
> Neither recalled nor changed shall be the command of my lips.

So Anshar summoned the gods to the Assembly and, after a
great banquet, they decided to enthrone Marduk as supreme
king.

O Marduk, thou art indeed our avenger.
We have granted thee kingship over the universe entire.
When in Assembly thou sittest, thy word shall be supreme.
Thy weapons shall not fail; they shall smash thy foes!

Conferring upon him all the insignia of kingship—scepter, throne, royal robe, matchless weapons—they raised the hymnic cry: "Marduk is king!"

The myth vividly describes Marduk's advance into battle in storm imagery echoed in Old Testament portrayals of Yahweh's epiphany with storm, thunder, and lightning (see Ps. 18; Nah. 1:3b–5; Hab. 3). Equipped with (rain)bow and arrows, the mace of the flood, and a net held by the four winds, the champion of the gods mounted his "storm-chariot irresistible and terrifying." A terrible struggle ensued. The other contestants stood back while Tiamat and Marduk came to grips in single combat to the death. When Tiamat—apparently conceived as a dragon or a fishlike monster—opened her mouth to swallow him,[12] Marduk drove into her the Evil Wind, causing her body to become distended, and while her mouth was wide open he shot an arrow into her inward parts.

> He released the arrow, it tore her belly,
> It cut through her insides, splitting the heart.
> Having thus subdued her, he extinguished her life.
> He cast down her carcass to stand upon it.

After chasing and capturing the entire rebel army, and recovering the Tablets of Fate from Kingu, Marduk returned to the

---

12 A. Heidel ([73], pp. 83–88) challenges the general view that Tiamat was a monster. While this may be debatable, other authorities join with him in insisting that the motif of a struggle between a god and a serpentine monster, as found in ancient Babylonian and Assyrian art, does not necessarily connect with the *Enuma elish* myth. The well-known seal, showing a god (Ninurta) slaying a seven-headed dragon (reproduced, for instance, in G. Ernest Wright, *Biblical Archaeology* [163], p. 102), is a heroic motif which stands by itself and has nothing to do with Marduk's combat (so Jacobsen).

huge corpse of Tiamat with the intention of establishing order, cosmos.

> Then the lord paused to view her dead body,
> That he might divide the monster and do artful works.
> He split her like a shellfish into two parts:
> Half of her he set up and ceiled it as sky,
> Pulled down the bar and posted guards.
> He bade them to allow not her waters to escape.

The other half became the "waters below," the watery abyss
upon which the earth rests and which encircles it (cf. Gen.
8:2). As the winds push back the threatening waters, so Marduk created the universe by making a separation of the upper
waters from the lower waters (cf. Gen. 1:6–7), interposing between the spheres a firmament equipped with locks and guards
(cf. Job 38:10). Half of Tiamat's body became the heaven, the
other half the earth. Marduk also created the sun, moon, and
stellar constellations to regulate the times and seasons.

The myth reaches a climax in Marduk's announcement of
his plan to build a house (temple) on earth, directly above the
waters of Apsu. For their part in the revolution, the rebel gods
were assigned the task of constructing Babylon with its great
temple Esagila. But lest the job of keeping this house fall on
the gods, Marduk conceived the idea of creating man.

> Blood I will mass and cause bones to be.
> I will establish a savage, "man" shall be his name.
> Verily, savage-man I will create.
> He shall be charged with the service of the gods
>   That they might be at ease!

Accordingly, the god Kingu, the commander of the rebel forces,
was brought to trial, condemned, and slain; and from his
blood, mixed with clay, man was created to be the slave of the
gods. The myth culminates with the gods assembled for a joy-
ous banquet in the temple of Babylon. There Anu pronounced
a blessing upon Marduk and invited the gods to proclaim

Marduk's fifty divine names, for "by however many names we call him, he is our god!" Thus it is affirmed that the powers of the major gods of the pantheon are found in their fullness in Marduk.

This myth reflects the new world order that came into being with the political ascendancy of the city of Babylon, especially under Hammurabi. The myth shows how Marduk overcame the powers of chaos by establishing the form of the state, whose center is Babylon, and whose king—like Marduk—is invested with the authority to establish and uphold order.[13] But the myth also expresses man's understanding of himself in the recurrent cycles of nature, within which he felt basically anxious and insecure. The annual devastation of the flooding Tigris and Euphrates rivers reminded men vividly that their ordered world was ever on the verge of chaos. "Every spring," writes Thorkild Jacobsen, "the waters flood the Mesopotamian plain and the world reverts to a—or rather to 'the'—primeval watery chaos until the winds fight the waters, dry them up, and bring back the dry land." In that situation men knew—with the passion of their existence, not with speculative or intellectual detachment—that they were "caught in an interplay of giant forces of nature." To them life had meaning only in relation to a cosmic realm in which "the potent truth of nature" majestically "disclosed itself." Hence the recitation of the myth and its accompanying ritual enactment brought men into contact with reality by involving them in the cosmic drama of the initial triumph of order against the menacing powers of chaos.[14]

---

[13] Jacobsen stresses that the crisis imposed on the gods the form of "primitive democracy"—a single ruler ruling through an assembly. See his essay "Primitive Democracy in Ancient Mesopotamia" [82]; also his *Ancient Ways to Meaning* (see Bibliography, No. 82).

[14] See Jacobsen's discussion in *The Intellectual Adventure* [52], Chapter V; also the introductory chapter on "Myth and Reality" by H. and H. A. Frankfort.

II

Gunkel was one of the first to assess the influence of this mythological tradition upon the Bible. In the Appendix to his book on creation and chaos he included translations of the Babylonian stories of the Creation and Flood. The importance of the creation-chaos motif in Babylonian religion prompted him to take a new look at numerous passages, from Genesis to the Apocalypse (Revelation) of John, in which this theme appears. The subtitle of his book *(eine religionsgeschichtliche Untersuchung)* shows that he was conducting an investigation from the standpoint of the history of religions. As he says in the Preface, he was not interested in taking a stand for or against partisan views current in church or academic circles. To use contemporary language, his approach was phenomenological. He "bracketed out" the question of the facticity of the creation and the psychological question of how Israel came to believe in God's creation of the world. His aim was to discern and describe the features of a particular religious outlook based on the experience of the struggle between order and chaos.

Parts of Gunkel's classic book are still up to date even after more than seventy years. Of course, later archaeological discoveries have expanded the horizons of the ancient Near Eastern world and this new knowledge has required modification of Gunkel's views at a number of points. In the late nineteenth century, when Babylonian culture was being rediscovered, it was tempting to assume that Israel took over the Babylonian creation myth concerning Marduk's victorious combat against the dragon Tiamat and her chaotic allies. But the picture, we now know, was more complex. Variations of the myth were known throughout the ancient world. In Egypt, man's life was dominated by the daily rising of the sun from Stygian darkness and by the annual overflowing of the Nile. His dependence upon these powers of nature was reflected in the identification of the Nile with the waters of chaos and the view that each day the sun initiated a new creation by defeating the powers of darkness and chaos.[15] And in Canaan, the immediate setting of Israel's life, the same kind of mythical thinking had an important place in religion.

Mythological texts from Ras Shamra (ancient Ugarit) on the coast of Syria, dating from about 1400 B.C. in their redacted form, portray the dramatic conflict between Baal, the storm-god manifest in thunder, lightning, and violent rainfall, and a formidable enemy known as Sea *(Yam)* or River *(Nahar)*. At the opening of the drama the deified sea, bent on seizing kingship over the gods, sends an insolent message to the supreme god, El, and the divine assembly, demanding the surrender of Baal. As in the Babylonian myth, the gods are helpless and sit despairingly with their heads dropped toward their knees. Baal, however, after rebuking the assembled gods, comes to the rescue and goes forth to challenge Sea to mortal combat.

> Then soars and swoops the mace in the hand of Baal,
> Even as an eagle in his fingers.
> It smites the head of Prince Sea,
> Between the eyes of River the Ruler.
> Sea collapses and falls to the ground;
> His strength is impaired;
> His dexterity fails.
> Baal drags Sea away and disperses him;
> He annihilates River the Ruler.[16]

In consequence of Baal's victory over the hostile waters, the cry is raised in the divine assembly, "Let Baal reign!"

There are striking affinities between Baal's role as portrayed in these texts and Marduk's role in the *Enuma elish* myth. In both cases a young deity battles and defeats a sea monster that embodies the powers of chaos, and in both cases the struggle is

---

[15] See especially John A. Wilson in *The Intellectual Adventure* [52], pp. 31–121; also Otto Kaiser, *Die mythische Bedeutung des Meeres in Aegypten, Ugarit und Israel* [86], ("The Mythical Significance of the Sea in Egypt, Ugarit, and Israel").

[16] Translated by John Gray, *The Legacy of Canaan* [66], p. 28; also in *Documents from Old Testament Times* [7], p. 129.

related to the establishment of kingly rule, that is, the kingdom of God.[17] A dominant theme of the Ras Shamra texts is Baal's "everlasting sovereignty."

> Behold, thine enemies, O Baal,
> Behold, thine enemies thou shalt smite,
> Behold, thou shalt subdue thine adversaries.
> Thou shalt take thine eternal kingdom,
> Thy sovereignty everlasting.

Also, the Ras Shamra texts, like the Babylonian story, relate the building of a temple for Baal in which the gods hold a great banquet to celebrate his winning the kingship.

Yet there are important differences too, though admittedly any evaluation is hampered by the fragmentary character of the Ras Shamra texts and the question of their proper order. A major difference is that the myth of Baal's victory over Sea and River is not explicitly connected with creation, unless "creation" is broadened out to include the preservation of the world.[18] Most Ras Shamra experts agree that the myth of Baal's victory over the waters has no connection with the theme of creation. Apparently Canaanites extolled El, the head of the pantheon, as creator; Baal, on the other hand, was responsible for maintaining the regularities of the earth in the face of menacing change and contingency. Canaanite mythology reflected the existential concerns of men in an agricultural milieu who felt themselves threatened by the powers of chaos during the cycle of the seasons. Baal's annual victory over the

---

[17] Since the sea does not dominate Mesopotamian consciousness, Jacobsen maintains that the motif of the combat with Sea was brought from Phoenicia, probably by the Amorites who, by 1750 B.C., had spread throughout Mesopotamia and had become the dominant element of the population of Canaan. A consequence of the migration of the myth, he says, is that Marduk took on Baal's characteristics as a god of lightning and storm. This view, expounded to me in conversation, will be set forth in Jacobsen's *Ancient Ways to Meaning* (see Bibliography, No. 82).

[18] The broader view is maintained by Loren R. Fisher in "Creation at Ugarit and in the Old Testament" [50]. He distinguishes between creation of the El type and creation of the Baal type and argues that Israel was influenced primarily by the latter since it spoke more directly to the problem of "their world and their own existence."

unruly waters, which established his dominion as "Lord of the earth," was apparently the basis of a New Year enthronement festival, held in the autumn. In this cultic situation, as John Gray observes, the myth was "not the first stammerings of a scientific cosmology, but the means whereby the community sacramentally experienced the triumph of their god over chaos, sustaining their faith in the power of Providence in the present and in the future with all its hazards." [19]

While our knowledge of the culture of the ancient Near East has widened, there is still much to be said for Gunkel's view that Israel was influenced by Mesopotamian traditions at an early period. It is very possible, as W. F. Albright has maintained, that traditions concerning "primeval history" in Genesis 1–11, such as creation and flood stories, were brought by patriarchal migrations into Palestine, where they were later blended with Canaanite mythology. [20] If Gunkel's discussion of the theme of "creation and chaos" needs modification it is primarily because we have come to a deeper understanding of the distinctive faith of Israel. To be sure, Gunkel insisted that what Israel took over was not slavishly copied; Israel transformed what she borrowed by baptizing it into her own faith. Yet our understanding of that faith has been enhanced by the method of form-criticism which Gunkel himself developed.

III

Gunkel died in the year 1932, precisely at the time when far-reaching theological changes were taking place. Here we cannot consider the impact of Karl Barth and Rudolf Bultmann,

---

[19] *The Legacy of Canaan* [66], p. 30. See also Gaster, "Cosmogony," in *The Interpreter's Dictionary of the Bible* [3].

[20] W. F. Albright, *From the Stone Age to Christianity* [9], pp. 237–38. Gunkel, arguing from internal biblical evidence, had maintained that Israel's assimilation of the foreign material required a long period of time. Albright supports Gunkel by relying on the external evidence provided by archaeology. See further Albright's remarks in the *Journal of Biblical Literature*, Vol. 58 (1939) where he takes this position in an argument with Mowinckel (pp. 91–103).

of Reinhold and Richard Niebuhr, of the martyred Dietrich Bonhoeffer and the lately deceased Paul Tillich, and many others whose creative thinking has added to the theological ferment of the past decades. In the field of Old Testament studies, where the revival of Biblical Theology has added to the theological ferment, scholars have come to broad agreement on one basic matter: the uniqueness of the Bible is that it takes history seriously as the sphere of God's self-disclosure and of man's authentic existence.[21] Indeed, if we may slip for a moment into Gunkel's history-of-religions context, it may now be said that it is the biblical sense of history which accounts for the singularity of Israel's faith in relation to other religions, ancient or modern. Other peoples of antiquity, to be sure, had some awareness of the dimension of history and could even speak of their gods as taking part in historical events.[22] But by and large the religions of Israel's neighbors were tied to the sphere of nature, where the cyclical rhythms were determinative for man's existence. Israel parted with the religions of the ancient Near East by declaring that history is the area of ultimate meaning precisely because God has chosen to make himself known in historical events and to call men to participate in his historical purpose. If today we share, to some degree, this historical consciousness—even in secularized versions—we are primarily debtors to the Israelites and their Christian heirs, not to the Babylonians, Egyptians, Canaanites, or Greeks. An eminent authority in the field of comparative

----

21 Beneath the surface of this consensus, however, are fundamental disagreements about what "history" means. For a perceptive treatment of this language problem see Will Herberg, "Five Meanings of the Word 'Historical' " [75]. The whole emphasis upon history in Biblical Theology has been sharply challenged by James Barr, "Revelation through History in the Old Testament and in Modern Theology" [16]; also, *Old and New in Interpretation* [17], Chap. 3.

22 The latent historical consciousness of Israel's neighbors has been stressed by Helmut Gese, "The Idea of History in the Ancient Near East and the Old Testament" [61]. On the subject of the ancient view of history in relation to the Old Testament, see further R. C. Dentan, ed., *The Idea of History in the Ancient Near East* [36]; see also Speiser, "The Biblical Idea of History in its Common Near Eastern Setting" [143].

religions, Mircea Eliade, writes: "The chief difference between
the man of the archaic and traditional societies and the man
of the modern societies with their strong imprint of Judaeo-
Christianity lies in the fact that the former feels himself in-
dissolubly connected with the Cosmos and the cosmic rhythms,
whereas the latter insists that he is connected only with History." [23]

Eliade's phenomenological studies have thrown great light
upon the significance of the motif of creation and chaos in a
mythical view of reality. The man of archaic societies, he
points out, has an "ontological thirst," that is, he thirsts for
reality, which can give meaning to his life. Like any of us, such
a man does not live by bread alone; he must find the meaning
of his existence. Yet paradoxically, this man "sees himself as
real, i.e. as 'truly himself' only and precisely insofar as he
ceases to be so" [24]—only as he flees from history into a change-
less, timeless realm. He experiences a deep nostalgia for the
security of what is ordained in nature, and therefore a longing
to participate through the cultus in the Great Time which
ever moves in a circle back to its beginning: a new creation.
True "being" is disclosed to him when history is "abolished"
and he is related to "an absolute reality" opposed to the profane world. [25]

According to this understanding, ancient man found himself existentially involved in the fateful drama of the annual
struggle between creation and chaos. For him the "sacred history"—if we may use the term *Heilsgeschichte* loosely—was essentially a cosmic drama which moves in a circle according to
the pattern: creation, lapse, restoration. In the beginning the

---

[23] Mircea Eliade, *Cosmos and History: The Myth of the Eternal Return*
[44], p. viii. See also Gerhard von Rad, *Old Testament Theology* [126],
Vol. II, pp. 110-12. The theological implications of Eliade's analysis are
discussed by Kenneth Hamilton, "*Homo Religiosus* and Historical Faith"
[70]; David L. Miller responds to this article, "*Homo Religiosus* and the
Death of God," in the same journal (Vol. XXXIV, pp. 305-15).

[24] M. Eliade [44], p. 34.

[25] *Ibid.*, p. 92.

creator-god conquered the powers of chaos and established order. But the powers of chaos were not completely eliminated and hence, under their persistent attack, time degenerates, confusion spreads, the world moves to the edge of chaos. Each year man, along with the cosmos, falls away from reality and must be purified and reborn. But at the turn of the New Year the victory over chaos is won again and the world is renewed.

In the Babylonian New Year festival the recitation of the *Enuma elish* myth was nòt just the telling of a popular story— "a fictitious narrative involving supernatural persons and embodying popular ideas on natural phenomena," to cite a modern dictionary definition. Rather, "the 'myth' (literally the 'word') is technically the spoken counterpart of ritual actions and has the purpose of making those explicit to the participants in the rites and of making those rites as acts of imitative magic doubly effective." [26] Accordingly, the recitation of the creation myth was part of a cultic reenactment in which worshipers participated in a "new creation," that is, a *repetition* of the original creation. The spoken word was the counterpart of a reenactment of the combat between Marduk and Tiamat by two groups of actors. This ritual action, Eliade points out, was not just a commemoration of the primordial victory: ". . . it repeated, it actualized, the cosmogony, the passage from chaos to cosmos. The mythical event was present: 'May he continue to conquer Tiamat and shorten her days!' the celebrant exclaimed. The combat, the victory, and the Creation took place *at that very moment.*" [27] In this way the worshiper participated in the power of primal reality which is unaffected by historical change and vicissitude. In another of his writings, *The Sacred and the Profane,* Eliade describes the act of pagan worship as a *reactualization* of creation:

> The participants in the festival become contemporaries of the mythical event. In other words, they emerge from their historical

---

[26] J. Gray, *The Legacy of Canaan* [66], p. 20.
[27] Eliade [44], p. 56.

time—that is, from the time constituted by the sum total of profane personal and intrapersonal events—and recover primordial time, which is always the same, which belongs to eternity.[28]

According to this view creation occurs cyclically as each old year declines and the new year comes round. There is nothing new under the sun.

Notice that this phenomenological study is directed to the mentality of "archaic man" wherever he may be found—in Babylonia, Anatolia, Canaan, Egypt, China, Russia, or America. When peoples are called to great historical responsibility they are easily overcome with historical weariness and wistfully long for some hiding place, some valley of Shangri-la hidden far up in the mountains of Tibet, where they may experience the virgin possibilities of life. We may pause to ask ourselves whether in our time, when one slip could mean the release of worldwide chaos and destruction, this longing for the peace and security of nature is not unusually potent. There may be a deep affinity between modern man and archaic man who, according to Eliade's analysis, could not find reality in historical change and catastrophe. He feared to "make history," to take upon himself the burden of freedom. So he retreated from "profane time" into "sacred time"—the time of the festivals. He absolved himself of historical responsibility by referring his major actions to the imitation of what the gods did in the beginning. He found salvation from "the terrors of history" by participating cultically in the security and stability of what is ordained in nature.

Against this background of comparative religion the faith of Israel stands out as a unique phenomenon—indeed, a revolutionary development. In contrast to religions which depreciate history and consequently dehistoricize man, the Bible sets forth a historical drama—a *Heilsgeschichte*—in which man becomes "truly himself" as a historical being who decides and acts in response to the action of God in history. Pannenberg states the contrast in these words: "Israel is distinguished by

---

[28] *The Sacred and the Profane* [45], p. 88.

the fact that it experienced the reality of its God not in the shadows of a mythical primitive history, but more and more decisively in historical change itself." [29] To be sure, Israel adopted the distinction between the sacred and the profane which was basic to all ancient religions, a distinction which is emphasized especially in Priestly theology. But in Israel's faith the realm of the sacred was located in the midst of history, not in some mythical twilight zone, for Israel experienced the reality of God in "concrete events and interpersonal relations." Instead of cultically imitating actions of the gods in "the olden days" beyond historical recall, Israel remembered and celebrated events that happened in a definite place and time. Consider the revolutionary impact of the announcement that in a political event—the Exodus from Egypt—the saving power of God was revealed!

> The Lord [Yahweh] said, "I have seen the affliction of my people who are in Egypt, and have heard their cry because of their taskmasters; I know their sufferings, and I have come down to deliver them out of the hand of the Egyptians, and to bring them up out of that land to a good and broad land, a land flowing with milk and honey."
>
> —EXODUS 3:7–8a

So Israel came to know the reality of God in the realm of the profane, the secular, the historical. And the consequence of this "knowledge of God"—to use a key term from the prophet Hosea (e.g. Hos. 4:1, 6)—was that the realm of nature, which ancient people regarded as sacred, was desacralized, or emptied of divinity. When the *Enuma elish* myth relates that Marduk seized from the rebel Kingu the Tablets of Fate which predetermined the courses of the stars, the pagan view is divulged that man's destiny is subject to the movement of the heavenly bodies, the divine powers of nature. From this standpoint man's interest in nature was that of the astrologer who anxiously observes the heavens in order to divine the predeter-

---

[29] Wolfhart Pannenberg, "Redemptive Event and History" [121], p. 316.

mined course of affairs. Israel, of course, knew her dependence
upon the rhythms of nature—"seedtime and harvest, cold and
heat, summer and winter, day and night" (Gen. 8:22). Under
the influence of the Canaanites her life came to be ordered by
the great agricultural festivals celebrated at the sanctuary three
times a year: at the time of the barley harvest, the first fruits
of wheat harvest, and the vintage at the year's end (Ex. 34:22–
23). But Israel broke with paganism, and its mythical view of
reality, at the crucial point: nature is not the realm of the
divine. The God Israel worships is the Lord of nature, but he
is not the soul of nature. Israel's sense of God's transcendence
resulted in "the emancipation of thought from myth."

> When we read in Psalm 19 that "the heavens declare the glory of
> God, and the firmament sheweth his handiwork," we hear a voice
> which mocks the beliefs of Egyptians and Babylonians. The
> heavens, which were to the psalmist but a witness of God's great-
> ness, were to the Mesopotamians the very majesty of godhead, the
> highest ruler, Anu. To the Egyptians the heavens signified the mys-
> tery of the divine mother through whom man was reborn. In
> Egypt and Mesopotamia the divine was comprehended as im-
> manent: the gods were in nature. The Egyptians saw in the sun
> all that a man may know of the Creator; the Mesopotamians
> viewed the sun as the god Shamash, the guarantor of justice. But
> to the psalmist the sun was God's devoted servant who "is as a
> bridegroom coming out of his chamber, and rejoiceth as a strong
> man to run a race." The God of the psalmists and the prophets
> was not in nature. He transcended nature—and transcended, like-
> wise, the realm of mythopoeic thought.[30]

Thus in Israel's faith nature was "disenchanted," to use language of the sociologist of religion Max Weber. This emancipation of nature from divine powers has had two major results.
In the first place, by enabling man to stand at a distance from
nature as an observer, calm and unafraid, it has encouraged
the development of natural science, as Harvey Cox has rightly
observed.[31] But this disenchantment has had another, and

---

[30] H. and H. A. Frankfort, *The Intellectual Adventure* [52], p. 363.
[31] Harvey Cox, *The Secular City* (New York: Macmillan, 1965) pp. 21–

equally important effect: it has opened the way for a new understanding of creation as a historical, rather than a mythical
account. This means, as M. H. Hartshorne has observed, "that
in contrast to paganism, which always regards nature as divine,
to be approached with awe and fear, Biblical faith saw the
world as the creature of God, its meaning and mystery derived
not from its hidden powers but from its role in the drama of
history of which God is Lord and Sovereign." [32]

IV

Even in an age of appalling biblical ignorance it is generally
known that the Bible opens with the affirmation "In the beginning God created the heavens and the earth." What often
escapes attention is that the creation story in Genesis 1:1—2:4a
and the supplementary account in Genesis 2:4b–25 are inseparably related to the historical narration which unfolds through
the period of the fathers of Israel (Gen. 12–50), the events of
the Exodus from Egypt and the invasion of Canaan (the books
of Exodus through Joshua and Judges), the rise and fall of the
Israelite nation (the books of Samuel and Kings) and—in the
Christian view—on to the denouement of the historical drama
in God's revelation in Jesus Christ. Often we detach "creation"
from this historical context and consider it as a separate "doctrine" (which happens usually in discussions of the relation
between science and religion). But this violates the intention
of the creation stories. They want to speak to us primarily
about history. Accordingly, the greatest weight must be given
to the form of these stories: they are "historical accounts" and,
as such, are part of the historical narration which moves from
the beginning toward the consummation of God's historical

---

24. He writes: "However highly developed a culture's powers of observation, however refined its equipment for measuring, no real scientific break-
through is possible until man can face the natural world unafraid. Wherever nature is perceived as an extension of himself or his group, or as the
embodiment of the divine, science as we know it is precluded."

32 M. H. Hartshorne, *The Promise of Science and the Power of Faith*
[72], pp. 85 f.

purpose. Indeed the question is in order as to whether it is proper to call these stories "myths"—though admittedly this term, defined in a subtle theological manner, has been used effectively by modern interpreters.[33] One does not necessarily have to rally to the standard of Barthian theology to agree with Barth's observation in the *Church Dogmatics* (III, 1) that, theologically, we should speak of creation not as myth but as *Sage* (the German word is best translated as "saga" rather than "legend"). In any case, the creation story has the same *historical concern* as the sagas found in Genesis 12–50 or the historical narration which dominates the book of Exodus.

Here it is appropriate to inquire into the hermeneutical implications of speaking of the creation stories as historical accounts. Some time ago I invited my colleague Will Herberg to our home to speak to a group of pastors about the biblical doctrine of creation. He began disarmingly by observing that in the Bible, creation is not a "doctrine" but an "account"; therefore, the way to understand the story is, first of all, to begin with an inquiry into *meaning* (which, of course, is what hermeneutics is all about). He made three points which I should like to restate, though absolving him from responsibility for the details of my elaboration. First, he said, *meaning can be predicated only of human occurrences.* We cannot interpret the rocks and the stars, as though nature had a meaning of its own; we can only describe these natural phenomena from the outside, i.e. scientifically. If the first chapter of Genesis has meaning for us, we have to treat it as an account of a historical occurrence, as a communication of a meaningful event from historical beings of the past to historical beings of the present.

---

33 An effective use of the term *myth* is found in M. H. Hartshorne [72], p. 85: "The Biblical account of creation is a myth, which means that it expresses the fundamental assumptions concerning the nature and meaning of human existence that the men of the Bible held. These are stated in mythological form because, like all basic presuppositions, they are beyond proof and explanation and rational explication: they describe the ground of all understanding and action. Implicit in faith, they point to and participate in the mystery of faith's ground, which can be stated only in story and song."

To be sure, in faith we insist that the Bible is not just a human book; it contains the Word of God and therefore it is sacred. Still, God's Word could become intelligible to men only as it was spoken in human words, only as it became concrete in human history. Thus to speak of the creation story as a historical account means, first of all, that it communicates to us historical meaning. And second, said Herberg, *meaning cannot be predicated of bare occurrences.* Meaning emerges when an event is interpreted, when it is proclaimed—just as the Exodus requires the presence of Moses as the prophet who declares its meaning. The inseparable connection between event and interpretation is indicated in Hosea's words:

> By a prophet Yahweh brought Israel up from Egypt,
>   and by a prophet he was preserved.
> —HOSEA 12:13

Moreover, to come to Herberg's third point, *an event may have several interpretations,* as in the case of Jesus' healings, which may be regarded as the works of Beelzebub, as psychosomatic cures, or as the signs of God's power. Which interpretation is used to endow an event with meaning, Herberg argued, depends on your underlying premise, your basic presuppositions, your fundamental orientation. These are the "fundamental assumptions" which—as Hartshorne has put it—"are beyond proof and explanation and rational explication" for "they describe the ground of all understanding and action." [34]

These three points illumine one of the major results of form-critical and traditio-historical research of the Hexateuch: the creation accounts at the beginning of the Bible are written from the standpoint of the meaning disclosed in the event of the Exodus. The history that is now recorded forwards must be read backwards, so to speak, through the faith of the believing community. And the fulcrum of Israel's faith, as it is expressed in the Hexateuch, is the event of the Exodus. In a profound sense the Bible does not really begin with Genesis but with Exodus, not with the first article of the creed ("I be-

---

[34] See footnote 33.

lieve in God . . . the Creator") but the second (historical redemption through his Servant).[35] Only by reference to the crucial event of the Exodus did Israel know who God is and
understand her calling as a people.

> I am Yahweh your God
> from the land of Egypt;
> you know no God but me,
> and besides me there is no savior.
>
> —HOSEA 13:4

In Israel's faith the meaning of the Exodus was universalized
so that it became the meaning of nature too, and therefore it
is proper to say that creation in the larger sense was "an infer-
ence from the experience of redemption" (J. C. Rylaarsdam).

Today it is widely recognized that Israel's oldest confession
of faith was a "historical credo," the content of which is preserved in Deuteronomy 26:5–10.

> A wandering Aramean was my father; and he went down into
> Egypt and sojourned there, few in number; and there he became
> a nation, great, mighty and populous. And the Egyptians treated
> us harshly, and afflicted us, and laid upon us hard bondage. Then
> we cried to Yahweh the God of our fathers, and Yahweh heard
> our voice, and saw our affliction, our toil, and our oppression; and
> Yahweh brought us out of Egypt with a mighty hand and an out-
> stretched arm, with great terror, with signs and wonders; and he
> brought us into this place and gave us this land, a land flowing
> with milk and honey. And behold, now I bring the first of the
> fruit of the ground, which thou, O Yahweh, hast given me.

It is interesting that this thanksgiving for the first fruits of the
ground is not connected with creation—with "the first article
of faith"—but rather with the saving deeds of Yahweh which
Israel had experienced.[36] This may seem strange when one considers that the liturgy is connected with an agricultural festi-

---

[35] See Claus Westermann, *A Thousand Years and a Day* [156], pp. 2–3.
In the same vein are his comments in *The Genesis Accounts of Creation*
[158], pp. 2–5.

[36] G. von Rad makes this observation in his commentary *Deuteronomy*
[125], p. 159.

val: the time of wheat harvest. But it is precisely in this confession that we find the seed of the creation-faith. Israel's faith was not based on mythical events recurring in nature, as in the agricultural Baal religion, but was rooted in the wonder of a historical event which evoked a people's praise. The "historical credo" fairly pulses with a kind of "ontological wonder"—the wonder of Israel's existence as God's people. Indeed, its basic structure corresponds to that of the hymn of praise in which the worshiping Israelite confesses the events by which God called his people into being and endowed them with a historical destiny (see Ps. 105).[37]

The Exodus was the time of Israel's creation *ex nihilo*—that is, when God in freedom acted to constitute a people in relationship with him. It is not accidental that the Second Isaiah, whose message recapitulates the Exodus tradition, speaks of Yahweh as Israel's creator and recalls the time when, at the Reed Sea, he acted to create. Moreover, in the "Song of the Sea" found in Exodus 15:1–18, a hymn which praises Yahweh for the mighty deeds by which he demonstrated his kingship, the deliverance at the Reed Sea is understood to be an act of the creation of Israel. This is evident from the Hebrew text of verse 16, which should be translated:

> Until thy people pass over, O Yahweh,
> until thy people pass over whom thou hast created.[38]
> —Exodus 15:16

Here we have an extremely early testimony, surely from the time of the early monarchy and possibly from the previous period of the Tribal Confederacy, concerning the historical wonder of Yahweh's creation of the community.[39] This sense

---

37 See C. Westermann, *The Praise of God in the Psalms* [157], pp. 115 f.

38 The RSV translates the verb *qānā* here as "purchase, acquire"; in the ancient poem in Deut. 32, however, the same verb clearly means "create" (Deut. 32:6). See further Paul Humbert, "*Qānā* en hébreu biblique" [80].

39 For a defense of the early date, "probably the twelfth century B.C.," see Frank M. Cross and David N. Freedman, "The Song of Miriam" [32]; and F. M. Cross, "The Divine Warrior in Israel's Early Cult" [35], pp.

of the wonder of Israel's being has found expression in many
songs of praise:

> Know that Yahweh is God!
> It is he that made us, and we are his;
> we are his people, and the sheep of his pasture.
> —PSALM 100:3

Studies of the history of Israel's tradition have helped us to
see that the biblical history, which now begins with the creation of the universe, is an expanded and developed expression
of Israel's historical faith as found in capsule form in the "historical credo." From the Exodus, Israel looked back to the
creation, confessing that the God who was active at the beginning of her history was likewise active at the beginning of the
world's history. This is the theological significance of Gerhard
von Rad's traditio-historical analysis of the Pentateuch, with
his threefold play on words which is possible only in German:
the *Einbau, Ausbau,* and *Vorbau*—that is, the "in-building" of
the Sinai traditions into the confessional story of Yahweh's
acts, the "building out" of the patriarchal traditions, and the
final step of "building before" the whole expanded history the
Urgeschichte or the primeval history. Even though von Rad's
analysis may give too much credit to the literary accomplishment of the "Yahwist" in the time of Solomon, he has helped
us to understand how the creation stories have become part of
the sacred history *(Heilsgeschichte)* which, in the present form
of the Hexateuch, begins with the call of Abraham.[40] From

22–23. James Muilenburg, in "A Liturgy on the Triumphs of Yahweh"
[114], favors a date in the early monarchy, while Marc Rozelaar, in "The
Song of the Sea" [137], broadly dates it between the time of David and
the Exile.

[40] Von Rad's position is set forth in the lead essay of his *The Problem
of the Hexateuch and Other Essays* [123] and in the introduction to his
commentary on *Genesis* [124]. More stress is placed on the formation of
the tradition in the premonarchic period by Martin Noth in his *Ueberlieferungsgeschichte des Pentateuch* [117]. An important evaluation of the
bearing of tradition-history upon Israel's early history and cultic practice
is the essay by Cross, "The Divine Warrior in Israel's Early Cult" [35].

the standpoint of Israel's faith, creation is the beginning of the action of God.

To portray the ultimate boundary of human history, that is, the creation, the biblical tradition makes use of traditional motifs which once circulated in pagan contexts with a completely different meaning. In the Priestly tradition, as Gunkel noted long ago, there is a faint echo of the old cosmogonic myth, known in ancient Babylonia, Egypt, Canaan, and elsewhere. As in the *Enuma elish* myth, Genesis 1 begins by portraying a precreation condition of watery chaos. Indeed, the Hebrew word for *deep* (Gen. 1:2: *Tehom*) appears here without the definite article (elsewhere it is in the feminine gender), as though it were a distant echo of the mythical battle with Tiamat, the female personification of the powers of chaos.[41] Just as Marduk used the winds as his weapons in the battle against the chaotic powers, so the Priestly account portrays the "spirit" or the "wind" of God raging over the face of the waters. And in the Priestly account, too, creation is portrayed as an act of "separation"—separation of primal light from primal darkness and separation of the "waters below" from the "waters above" by interposing a firmament (Gen. 1:3–8). Of course, the waters of chaos are no longer regarded as rebellious powers of evil over which the creator must gain a victory. Nevertheless, there is still a distant echo of the old mythical view that the universe was created by making a space between the chaotic waters. In Priestly tradition, this view reappears in the Flood story. According to this version of the story, the Flood was almost a cosmic catastrophe, for the waters poured in through the "sluices of *Tehom* ["Deep"]" and through the "windows of heaven," thus threatening the return of the earth to chaos (Gen. 8:2). In the Yahwist epic (Gen. 2–3) this chaos motif does not appear in the same way. The *'ed* ("flood") which rises

---

41 It is generally recognized that there is a linguistic relation between Hebrew *Tehom* and Babylonian Tiamat. For an exegetical discussion of Gen. 1:1–2, see especially Brevard Childs, *Myth and Reality in the Old Testament* [27], pp. 30–42. Heidel, in *The Babylonian Genesis* [73], Chap. III, discusses affinities and differences between the *Enuma elish* and the account in Gen. 1.

from the ground to water its surface (Gen. 2:6) is not the hostile water of chaos but rather the sweet subsoil water, from which come "the blessings of *Tehom* ["Deep"]" (Gen. 49:25). In this story the contrast is not between cosmos and chaos but between a well-watered oasis and the surrounding wilderness where the soil yields its produce grudgingly.

These traditional motifs have been torn out of their pagan contexts and placed into a completely new context of meaning: the history of God's dealings with Israel. While the Priestly story of creation utilizes the old chaos motif, it does not intend to present the view of a cyclical lapse from the Great Time of the beginning and a periodic struggle between order and chaos. Rather, this traditional material is used poetically to portray the absolute beginning of history. The intention of adding the Yahwist's story of Paradise Lost as a supplement was to say that the lapse occurred once, at the beginning, and thereby provided the background and presupposition of God's purposeful activity in human history through his people, Israel.

To summarize: The biblical account of creation with which the Bible opens is governed by a historical intention, even when it uses materials that were formerly mythical in their presuppositions. Here creation does not stand by itself: it is inseparably related to and a part of history. In order to confess faith in God, the Lord of history, Israel traced the purpose of Yahweh back into patriarchal times, thereby declaring that her God is "the God of Abraham, Isaac, and Jacob." And, not content to stop with the prehistory of Israel, she traced that same sovereignty back beyond the patriarchal times into primeval history, though in this realm she was guided only by theological conviction, not by historical recollection.[42] Using traditional materials, Israel filled out the content of prehistorical

---

[42] Bruce Vawter, discussing the "historical sense" in the book of Gen., writes of the period of primeval history: "The description of this age is done by conviction [based on Israel's encounter with Yahweh in the time of Moses and the Exodus] rather than remembrance." See his essay "Understanding Genesis" [150], pp. 60 f.

times and, in faith, reached the boundary of history: the beginning. When one considers the intrinsic relation between creation and history in Israel's faith, the cogency of these words by Ludwig Köhler becomes inescapable:

> The creation of the world by God in the Old Testament is no independent fact; creation is intended to be the opening of history. The Old Testament history of creation does not answer the question "How did the world come into being?" with the answer: "God created it," but answers the question "From where does the history of God's people derive its meaning?" with the answer: "God has given the history of His people its meaning through creation." In other words, *the Creation in the Old Testament does not belong to the sphere of natural science but to the history of man.*[43]

This means that creation is an article of faith for which there is no scientific support precisely because creation is not, biblically speaking, a natural event, but a historical event. Insofar as the biblical account portrays the natural world, the setting of human history, there are inevitable clashes with science: the three-storied view of the universe; the view that the whole process occurred in six days; the creation of light before the luminaries. But these matters are not the substance of the account. In its biblical context this whole story, considered as a poetic unity, intends to trace the origin and meaning of history back to the creative, sovereign will of God, the Lord of all times from beginning to end, from first things to last things. Creation is "the beginning of history"; it is this conviction—not ingenious mathematical calculation—which motivates Jews to begin their calendar with the presumed date of the creation of the world.[44] According to biblical faith, our historical existence is enfolded within the plan and purpose of the God who is not a phenomenon of history but the Lord of history, who

---

43 Ludwig Köhler, *Old Testament Theology* [89], p. 87.

44 See Edmund Jacob, *Theology of the Old Testament* [81], pp. 136–42, where it is maintained that faith in God the creator is secondary to faith in God the savior and that the Old Testament creation-faith receives its orientation from the covenant.

is not a power immanent in nature but the sovereign Creator—
the God whose purpose and presence were made known in Israel's historical experience and in the fullness of time, according to Christian faith, in Jesus Christ.

2

Creation and Covenant

ONE OF THE RESULTS of our increasing knowledge of the culture of the ancient Near East is the new awareness of the importance of creation in the religions of Babylonia, Canaan, Egypt, and other countries. W. F. Albright, in his monumental work *From the Stone Age to Christianity,* has shown that in the Late Bronze Age (1500–1200 B.C.) the religions of the area had already ascribed cosmic and universal sovereignty to their great deities and that there were already advanced tendencies toward a kind of monotheism, as evidenced particularly in the monotheistic cult of the sun sponsored by the reforming Pharaoh Akhnaton (or Amenhotep IV: 1370–1353 B.C.). Since we have already stressed the role of the creator in Babylonian mythological texts, and have given some attention to the Ras Shamra mythology of Canaan, it is appropriate at the introduction of this chapter to discuss briefly the place of creation in the religion of ancient Egypt.

I

In contrast to Mesopotamia, where the fury of the thunderstorm and the turbulence of the great rivers at spring flood reminded men of the precariousness of their existence, the reli-

gion of Egypt was dominated by a serene sense of the orderly
cosmos as evidenced in the daily circuit of the sun, the rhythm
of the seasons, and the fertilizing of the earth by the annually
overflowing Nile. The "cosmic gods" who manifested themselves in the benevolent powers of nature were praised as the
source of the order and stability of the universe. In a hymn
(fifteenth century B.C.) to Amon, the god of the wind who was
worshiped at Thebes, the deity was praised as the source of life
in gods, men, and beasts:

> Thou greatest of heaven, thou oldest of the earth, lord of what
> exists . . .
> Legitimate lord, father of the gods, who created man and made
> the animals . . .
> Who made the upper ones and the lower ones, who illumines
> the two lands . . .
> Whose sweet odor the gods love, as he comes from Punt, rich in
> fragrance as he comes from the land of the Matoi, with fair
> countenance as he comes from "God's Land [Asia]". . .
> Praise to thee who didst create the gods, who didst raise heaven
> and stretch out the earth! [1]

In Memphis, another great Egyptian center, there developed
a sophisticated theology which proclaimed that Ptah, the power
in the earth, is a transcendent deity who created by his word.
Back of everything that exists is the will of the creator, who
first thought "in his heart" and then objectified his thought by
expressing it in creative command.

> Indeed, all the divine order really came into being through what
> the heart thought and the tongue commanded. . . . Thus were
> made all work and all crafts, the action of the arms, the movement
> of the legs, and the activity of every member, in conformance with
> (this) command which the heart thought, which came forth through
> the tongue, and which gives value to everything.[2]

---

[1] Quoted by William F. Albright, *From the Stone Age to Christianity*
[9], p. 214. See the whole discussion, pp. 209-36.
[2] Trans. by John A. Wilson, *Ancient Near Eastern Texts* [5], p. 5.

This lofty teaching reminds one of the psalmist's announcement:

> By the word of the Lord the heavens were made,
>   and all their host by the breath of his mouth.
>
> .   .   .   .
>
> For he spoke, and it came to be;
>   he commanded, and it stood forth.
>
> —PSALM 33:6, 9

—or the Priestly account in Genesis 1 with its recurring refrain: "And God said, 'Let there be . . .' And it was so." But this teaching about Ptah's transcendent power, by which the world in its fulness was established once and for all, was exceptional, as Henri Frankfort points out; for it was never able to displace the dominant view that the divine was "immanent in nature," whether in the wind (Amon) or the sun (Re), or the combined power of both acknowledged as one: Amon-Re, the supreme god of the Egyptian Empire.[3]

However, it was preeminently the sun-god, Re, who was celebrated as creator in Egyptian texts. For our purpose it is important to notice that Re did not create the existing order by triumphing over the powers of chaos in the beginning. To be sure, it could be said that creation took place in the primeval waters of Nun, or that the sun-god began his creation upon a hill which rose up out of the waters of chaos.[4] But these primeval waters apparently were passive, not active or insurgent. According to Egyptian mythology, the sun-god had to gain a daily victory over another kind of enemy: the power of darkness symbolized by the mythical dragon or serpent, Apophis.

---

3 Henri Frankfort, *Ancient Egyptian Religion* [54], pp. 20–24. See also J. A. Wilson's discussion of Egyptian mythopoeic thought in *The Intellectual Adventure* [52], Chaps. II–IV.

4 See the texts translated by Wilson in *Ancient Near Eastern Texts* [5], pp. 3–6. In note 7 he remarks: "Any important cult-center was regarded by the Egyptians as potentially a place of creation and therefore had its own hill of creation, symbolized in its holy of holies." On the subject of Primeval Hill and the surrounding waters of chaos, see further H. Frankfort, *Kingship and the Gods* [53], pp. 151 ff.

Each day, it was believed, the sun-god traveled in his boat through the skies above, and at night he journeyed through the underworld where he had to repulse the serpent. Each rising of the sun, then, was a new sign of the sun's triumph over the power of darkness.

> Thou risest, thou risest brilliantly;
> Thou art victorious over thy enemies;
> Thou causest the day-boat to sail past
> And repellest the dragon of the storm at nighttime;
> He cannot approach at the decisive moment;
> Thou hast destroyed the power of the enemies;
> The antagonists of Re are overthrown by the flame of terror.[5]

But this occurrence is, so to speak, part of the day's routine. It is part of the established regularity of the universe—not the sign of a theogonic strife which fundamentally threatens the cosmos. As Frankfort observes, the victory celebrated here is not so much an "achievement" as a "foregone conclusion"; for, in contrast to the Babylonian creation myth, in which everything hangs on the outcome of the battle between the creator and the powers of chaos, "the thought that risks were entailed, that an issue was at stake, is never allowed to arise." Consequently we find here not "epic grandeur" but "static splendor." [6]

This "static splendor" resulted from the fundamental conviction that endowed Egyptian culture with extraordinary tranquility and stability, namely, the social order exists within a cosmic order that is eternally permanent. To live rightly,

---

[5] Cited by Frankfort, *Ancient Egyptian Religion* [54], p. 133. See also "The Repulsing of the Dragon and the Creation," trans. Wilson in *Ancient Near Eastern Texts* [5], pp. 6–7.

[6] Frankfort [54], p. 133. See the illuminating discussion of the role of the king in the ritual reenactment of the creation by Paul Ricoeur, *The Symbolism of Evil* [132], Pt. II, Chap. I. He points out that whereas Egyptian mythology pictures the creator serenely rising out of the primeval ocean to form the world he was to rule, in Babylonian mythology creation is the final episode of a long conflict and "thus the divine monarchy itself is the product of confusion and anxiety." He maintains that the kingship in Babylonia reflects "the anguish arising from the instability of order."

according to Egyptian teaching, is to live in harmony with *Maat,* that is, the "order," "truth," "justice" ordained at creation. So intrinsic to reality was order in Egyptian religion that it would have been superfluous, if not utterly inconsistent, to portray a great creation drama of a theogonic strife in the beginning: a struggle within the realm of the divine itself against primordial powers of chaos and the emergence of order as a result of the creator's victory. Admittedly, it was said that at "the first time" (the creation), Re "put order *(Maat)* in the place of chaos," but this statement only emphasizes that the present cosmic order rests upon a foundation that is everlastingly sure and permanent. Accordingly, it was claimed that Pharaoh, who was extolled as the divine successor of the creator, champions "order" or "justice." In a positive sense, his rule mediated the divine order which brought welfare and blessing to the people. In a negative sense, he destroyed the criminals who rebelled against the royal authority, or crushed the enemies of Egypt who violated the orderly design of the universe—a role which is portrayed on the walls of ancient Egyptian temples in scenes where the gigantic Pharaoh is shown annihilating the enemies, "the powers of chaos." Thus the doctrine of creation, frequently mentioned in Egyptian texts, reflects "an attitude of mind which comprehended the universe as essentially static."

> Movement and change were not denied to exist, of course; but change, in so far as it was significant, was recurrent change, the life rhythm of a universe which had gone forth, complete and unchanging, from the hands of its creator. The alternation of night and day, of drought and inundation, of the succession of the seasons, were significant changes; their movement was part of the established order of creation. But single occurrences, odd events, historical circumstances were ephemeral, superficial disturbances of the regularity of being and for that reason unimportant.[7]

This conception of a society harmoniously integrated within a cosmic order was at home in the Nile Valley, but it could not

---

[7] Frankfort [54], pp. 49 f.; see the entire discussion of "Change, Permanence, and the conception of Maat," pp. 49–58.

be exported easily to Canaan where the powers of nature appeared to be more unruly, if not capricious. Israel, with her acute historical sense, was much more influenced by Canaanite portrayals of the divine epiphany with thunder, lightning, and rainstorm, or even the dramatic portrayal of the struggle between creation and chaos in Babylonian mythology.

Ironically, the one Egyptian testimony to creation which significantly influenced Israelite tradition was a writing which Egyptian orthodoxy dismissed as heretical, namely, the famous "Hymn to the Sun" allegedly composed by Pharaoh Akhnaton. This king apparently wanted to get rid of much of the mythology associated with the worship of the sun-god, Amon-Re, and to emphasize divine immanence by adoring the Aton, the disk of the sun, as the manifestation of God. By insisting upon the sole worship of the Aton, he challenged the polytheism of Egypt. His monotheistic zeal incurred such hostility that shortly after his death every trace of his reform was eradicated. The "Hymn to the Sun" is the king's adoration of the sun disk, the sole creator and renewer of life. It has long been recognized that this hymn is similar in spirit and even in wording to Psalm 104, suggesting Egyptian influence upon Israel's psalmody, probably by way of Israel's sages during the period of the early monarchy. Like Psalm 104, the Egyptian hymn is cast in the form of a prayer:

Thou appearest beautifully on the horizon of heaven,
Thou living Aton, the beginning of life!
When thou art risen on the eastern horizon,
Thou hast filled every land with thy beauty.
Thou art gracious, great, glistening, and high over every land;
Thy rays encompass the lands to the limit of all that thou has made.
. . . .
How manifold it is, what thou hast made!
They are hidden from the face (of man).
O sole god, like whom there is no other!
Thou didst create the world according to thy desire,
Whilst thou wert alone:
All men, cattle, and wild beasts,

Whatever is on earth, going upon (its) feet,
And what is on high, flying with wings.[8]

II

Considering the impressive evidences of the importance of the
creation-faith in pagan religions during the second millennium
B.C., it is curious that in Israel's faith during its formative and
creative period (1300–1000 B.C.) the belief in Yahweh as creator
apparently had a secondary place. To be sure, this statement
has to be made with due caution owing to the difficulty of
penetrating to the earliest layers of Israel's tradition. Even at
best our knowledge of this formative period is partial and
fragmentary, and often only conjecture is possible. It is noteworthy, however, that in early Israelite poetry the belief in
Yahweh as creator is not stressed. For example, the "Song of
Deborah" (Judg. 5), which comes from the latter part of the
twelfth century B.C. and displays striking affinities with Canaanite style,[9] misses a golden opportunity to mention Yahweh's power as creator in connection with his epiphany in an
earth-shaking storm for the purpose of delivering his embattled
people at Taanach by the waters of Megiddo. Here, however,
the poet highlights "the saving acts of Yahweh" (RSV, vs. 11
"triumphs") on behalf of his people Israel in a critical hour
of history. Or, in the "Song of Moses" (Deut. 32), which in its
earliest form may date back into the period before the Israelite
monarchy,[10] the poet praises Yahweh as creator but he means
specifically Yahweh's creation of his people, an event which
throws into sharp relief Israel's turning to "new gods that had
come in of late":

---

8 Trans. by Wilson in *Ancient Near Eastern Texts* [5], pp. 369 ff. For
further discussion of Akhnaton's reform, see Georg Steindorff and Keith
C. Seele, *When Egypt Ruled the East* [144], Chap. XIV.

9 W. F. Albright ("The Song of Deborah in the Light of Archaeology" [10]) dates the poem ca. 1125 B.C. and emphasizes its affinities with
Canaanite style.

10 See G. Ernest Wright, "The Lawsuit of God," [164].

Do you thus requite Yahweh,
    you foolish and senseless people?
Is not he your father, who created [qānā] you,
    who made you and established you?
                                        —DEUTERONOMY 32:6

And, to take one more example from early poetry, the "Song
of the Sea" (Ex. 15:1–18) praises Yahweh's victory in language
which at times sounds like the myth of the battle with the waters of chaos. But it is quite clear that in this old hymn the
enemy is Pharaoh's host, not the "deeps" (*tehomoth*, vss. 5, 8),
sea (vss. 8, 10), or "mighty waters" (vs. 10). As we have seen
(on p. 37), the only reference to creation in this hymn is the
affirmation concerning the creation of Israel.[11]

Furthermore, studies aimed at tracing the history of tradition within the Pentateuch (or Hexateuch) have drawn attention to the fact that the earliest summaries of Israel's faith did
not refer to Yahweh as creator but concentrated rather on the
mighty deeds of history by which he made himself known and
constituted Israel to be his people. The little historical credo
preserved in Deuteronomy 26:5–9 (see above, pp. 36 f.) could
have at least mentioned the creation-faith, for the confession
was made in connection with the offerings of the first fruits to
Yahweh at the time of the wheat harvest. But, as we have already seen, in this affirmation of faith the Israelite worshiper
speaks only of Yahweh's wondrous historical deeds which cli-
maxed in his leading Israel into the land. And finally, it is
striking that the northern (E) tradition begins with Abraham,
whereas the southern (J) tradition begins with the creation.
Although it is possible that the E tradition of primeval history
has been dropped, it is more plausible to assume that E has
merely followed the early formulation of Israel's faith and that

---

11 Frank M. Cross observes ("The Divine Warrior" [35], p. 16): "The
earliest sources do not equate the crossing of the sea and the killing of the
Dragon by the Divine Warrior, but it is highly likely that the role of the
sea in the Exodus story was singled out and stressed precisely because of
the ubiquitous motif of the cosmogonic battle between the creator god
and Sea in West Semitic mythology." The second part of that sentence becomes very illuminating if the first part is given its due emphasis.

in the J tradition this given outline was expanded by adding the creation story.

This reticence about creation cannot be explained as a weakness of Israel's faith in the period of the Tribal Confederacy, as though Yahweh had not yet taken over the realm of nature. Israelites knew and confessed that the God who was mighty in history was also able to make the powers of nature serve his purpose. He prepared a path for his people through the Reed Sea, preserved them during the wilderness sojourn by giving food and water, and rescued their army at the Battle of Megiddo by causing the stars to fight on their side and the river Kishon to overflow its banks. To Israel the very name "Yahweh" signified unlimited divine sovereignty. W. F. Albright and his students have vigorously supported the view that the Tetragrammaton (the sacred Name, Yahweh) is a causative imperfect of the proto-Hebrew verb *hwy*, and that it means "he causes to be," thus "he creates." In an illuminating article on the religion of the patriarchal period,[12] Frank Cross has given the argument a new twist by proposing that *yahweh* is an abbreviated form of a sentence-name which was a cultic epithet of El, the whole sentence being *yahwê ṣebā'ôt:* "he who creates the (heavenly) armies." This name, he theorizes, was the title of "the divine warrior and creator" and was akin in meaning to other titles applied to El in Canaan, like "father of the gods" or "creator of creatures." And this epithet was appropriated for Israel's use not just as a "creation formula," but as "the name of the god who led Israel in her historical wars." In this connection we may recall the "Song of Deborah," where Yahweh mobilizes "the stars in their courses" (the heavenly hosts) to fight against Sisera (Judg. 5:20), though the expression "Yahweh Sebaoth" does not appear in the song, and indeed is first mentioned explicitly in connection with the amphictyonic sanctuary of Shiloh (I Sam. 4:4).

Whatever the merits of this hypothesis, the study itself is a clear indication that it is no longer possible to accept the old

---

12 F. M. Cross, "Yahweh and the God of the Patriarchs" [34].

evolutionary view that Israel arrived at the doctrine of creation late, when her maturing faith flowered into the monotheism of Second Isaiah. The creation-faith was at least incipient in the Exodus-faith: in Israel's experience of the wonder of her being, in the spontaneous praise of the God who with almighty grace delivered his people from bondage to the mightiest empire of the day, in the awareness of Yahweh's unlimited sovereignty. Moreover, it would be strange indeed if Israel had taken no account of a belief which figured prominently in the religions of the cultural environment. As we have seen, the cultic drama which reactualized the cosmic struggle between order and chaos was fundamental to much ancient religion, and doubtless Israel was influenced by this view at a very early period.[13] During the period of the Tribal Confederacy (1200–1000 in round numbers) Israel adopted from Canaan the major agricultural festivals (cf. Ex. 34:22–23) which were tied up with the rhythms of nature. This festal calendar bears tacit witness to the influence of mythical views prevalent in the Near East, even though Israel converted the annual festivals into celebrations of the unique events of her history.

Considering all this, Israel's apparent reticence about creation in her early traditions needs to be accounted for. It is plausible to understand this reticence as a reaction against the creation-faith which was tied up with a mythical view of reality. It was not just that in the early period the creation-faith was secondary to the kerygma of historical redemption. The matter must be put more strongly. Israel, in reaction to the

---

13 John Gray maintains that the influence of the Canaanite version of the conflict with the powers of chaos was first felt in Egypt, and particularly in Baal-Saphon in the area of Goshen (Ex. 14:2) where the people encamped during their exodus. He argues that this was a cult center of Baal, as shown by the name of the place and by archaeological references, and that the local cult legend of Baal's triumph over the waters would have made an impact there. See his article "Canaanite Mythology and Hebrew Tradition" [67]. The Canaanite character of this place has also been emphasized by Otto Eissfeldt, *Baal Zaphon, Zeus Kasios und der Durchzug der Israeliten durchs Meer* [41]. Even granting all of this, however, it is doubtful whether the stay at this place was long enough to make such a profound impression.

prevailing nature religions, *gave* the belief a secondary place. This point is recognized by Frank Cross in a brief remark in a footnote which is so important that it should be elevated to the main text and italicized: "The radical novelty of Israel's early faith was its attempt to shift this center [the centrality of the drama of creation in Near Eastern cults] from creation to historical redemption in the cultic life of the nation." [14]

It must not be supposed that "the radical novelty of Israel's faith," which resulted in a shift of focus from creation to history, burst upon the whole Israelite community like a lightning flash. The "religion of Israel" as practiced in the early period was not coextensive with "the faith of Israel" as expressed normatively in the confessions or credos around which the traditions were eventually organized. If we knew more about the Israelite cult as practiced during the period of the Judges, for example at the El Berith (Baal Berith) temple in Shechem (see Judg. 9), we might discover that the celebration of Yahweh's kingship in terms of a dramatic struggle between order and chaos had an important place. It is hard to believe that the many allusions to the struggle with the dragon of chaos (Rahab, Leviathan, the Serpent, Sea, Floods) were only imported later to serve as poetic metaphors for the Yahweh faith.[15] It is more plausible that the motif of the struggle with chaos was carried along on the stream of Israel's religion from early times and only gradually was absorbed into her historical faith. Indeed, the absorption was never complete. One of the strange things about the biblical tradition is that, despite the power of Israel's faith to transform what it took over by making it serve such historically oriented themes as election, cove-

---

14 "Yahweh and the God of the Patriarchs" [34], p. 253, footnote 123. See also his essay "The Divine Warrior" [35], pp. 16–18, where he argues that mythic elements were present in the cult of the Confederacy, "standing in tension with themes of historical memory or enhancing redemptive events by assimilating them to cosmic events." "It is this *subdued mythological element* [italics mine]"—evident especially in archaic psalmody—"that breaks out afresh in the cultus and ideology of the monarchy."

15 The old view of creation as the outcome of a struggle with the primeval monster is echoed metaphorically, for instance, in Pss. 74:12–17; 89:9–13; Isa. 51:9–10; Job 7:12; 9:13; 26:10–13; 38:8–11.

nant, or promise and fulfillment, this "ancient Near Eastern ideology," as it has been called, was never fully eliminated. As we shall see in later chapters, the motif of creation versus chaos persisted in the Israelite cult, and eventually the imagery was revived in apocalyptic portrayals of the cosmic scale of the conflict between the Creator and the Adversary. Doubtless it was in the cult that this chaos imagery became so firmly fixed in Israelite life and thought that long after its original cultic meaning was forgotten it survived as poetic metaphor to add depth and richness to the expression of faith in Yahweh.

Although our knowledge of the history of Israelite worship is exceedingly limited, it is quite likely that the period before the monarchy was a time when the creation-faith and the Exodus-faith existed side by side without being harmonized completely, just as the worship of Baal as the lord of fertility and the worship of Yahweh as the leader of Israel's historical wars coexisted in uneasy tension. Even the worship of El, the high god of the Canaanite pantheon who was extolled as "creator of creatures," was not necessarily identical with Yahweh, the God who brought his people out of Egypt, though in Genesis 14:22–24 Abraham is pictured as equating Yahweh with El Elyon, "creator of heaven and earth." [16] When the periodic covenant-renewal ceremonies were held "before Yahweh" at the central sanctuary, and when the tribes of Israel, after hearing the story of Yahweh's acts, were asked to reaffirm their loyalty to Yahweh and to put away "strange gods" (see Josh. 24), this was undoubtedly an occasion for shifting the fulcrum from the creation-faith of Near Eastern cults to historical redemption. For Israel was constituted and bound together as a community on the basis of a "shared history" of holy events, preeminently the Exodus and its sequel, the entrance into the land. Therefore when the people came together to celebrate the great Israelite festivals, at Shechem or Shiloh, at Gilgal or Bethel, they were not invited to participate cultically in the

---

[16] Gen. 14, which stands outside the main traditions of the Pentateuch (J, E, D, P), will be discussed later in connection with possible Jebusite influence on Davidic theology.

ever-recurring "new creation," the annual triumph of cosmos over chaos; rather, they remembered and rehearsed the crucial events which were the basis of their life as a people and in terms of which they acknowledged who God is and what he requires. Thus the Israelites introduced at formerly Canaanite places a radically new style of worship, though one which was influenced by its cultural surroundings. The liturgical revolution had as its consequence, according to Martin Noth, that "the specifically Israelite reference to the exodus from Egypt now took the place of the ancient Near Eastern reference to the creation of the world." [17]

If the creation-faith was actually given a secondary place in Israel's early cult, the silence about creation in the ancient creedal confessions (e.g. Deut. 26:5–9) is not surprising. In the Israelite festivals such heavy emphasis was placed upon Yahweh's deeds in history (Heilsgeschichte) that creation was a central theological concern only in the sense of the creation of the people, that is, creation as a historical event. Before creation in the cosmic sense could become a central concern for Israelite worship, the creation-faith had to be demythologized, that is, divested of its mythical presuppositions and positively related to the soteriological drama of the Yahweh faith.[18]

III

The two creation stories at the beginning of the Bible bear witness to the outcome of this struggle. The story of creation, according to both P and J, was related theologically to Israel's Heilsgeschichte and thus became a historical account of the opening of the historical drama. However, we should like to

---

[17] Martin Noth, "God, King, People in the Old Testament" [119], p. 39. See also his essay on "The 'Re-presentation' of the Old Testament in Proclamation" [118], especially pp. 80–85.

[18] See Gerhard von Rad, "The Theological Problem of the Old Testament Doctrine of Creation" in his collected essays [123]. He maintains that in "genuinely Yahwistic belief" the doctrine of creation was not permitted to become an independent doctrine but was "incorporated into the complex of soteriological thought."

know more about how and when Israel historicized the crea-tion-faith. What brought about the change from reticence con-cerning creation to attempts to convert the creation-faith to the service of Israel's election-faith? Under what circumstances did the belief in creation cease being secondary to Israel's faith and come to be integrally related to the "shared history" of the believing community?

One explanation is that the creation-faith was emphasized as Israel's political horizons widened. In the early period Yah-weh's power, while unlimited, was sensed primarily within the sphere of Israel's historical existence, or perhaps was experi-enced in the context of the cult. The Lordship of Yahweh was expressed and acknowledged in terms of the history as Israel lived it, as in the "Song of Deborah" (Judg. 5). Only as Israel was drawn out of her comparatively restricted sphere into a larger historical arena, where great nations were vying to mas-ter the ancient world, did the horizons of faith enlarge. Then the time became ripe for Israel's sense of the absolute claim of Yahweh's will, as expressed in the First Commandment (Ex. 20:3), to expand in ever-widening circles: to the neighboring peoples, to the great nations and empires, to all mankind, to the whole realm of nature. Thus the belief in Yahweh as crea-tor represents the final extension of his historical sovereignty.

This explanation, it seems to me, is correct as far as it goes. Israel's transition from a Tribal Confederacy to a state under Davidic leadership was a momentous step which brought far-reaching changes in theological understanding. Von Rad may have oversimplified the matter by saying that the change was from life in the cultic sphere to life in the political sphere. In his commentary on Genesis he points out that the Yahwist (J), living in the time of the United Monarchy, faced a theological problem of the first magnitude. The old Israelite traditions had been created and formed within the cult. For *ancient* Is-rael believed that Yahweh spoke and acted in the cultic sphere: the sphere of the sacred festivals, of sacrifice and priestly lot, or of holy war when "the terror of God" would fall miracu-lously upon the enemy. But in the period of David, he says, this cultic cocoon was stripped away from the traditions; "it is as though they had changed into a chrysalis and now emerged in new, free form." The theological result, as we see it in the Yahwist epic, is nothing short of revolutionary. Israel's traditions are desacralized, for the Yahwist sees Yahweh's activity in the profane sphere of life—"in the facts of history as in the quiet course of a human life, in the sacred things but not less in the profane, in great miracles as well as in the innermost secrets of the human heart." [19] So Israel, emancipated from the cultic limitations of the Confederacy, found her horizons widened as never before; Yahweh's sovereignty was experienced in more spacious ways. If we take our cue from this interpretation, creation too was "secularized." The creation-faith was taken out of the cult, so to speak, and was made part of the preface (Vorbau) to the Heilsgeschichte in order to show that all men are embraced within Yahweh's sovereign purpose and that secular history, from its very beginning, has its origin and meaning in his sovereign will.

This interpretation goes a long way toward helping us to understand the way the creation-faith was brought into the context of Israel's historical faith, though one may add the caveat that the picture of faith bursting from a cultic cocoon and taking wings in the free, secular air is somewhat overdrawn. But there is still much that is unexplained. Granting that the formation of the Yahwist epic around the theological core of the old cultic credo was an "astonishing creative, accomplishment," we may legitimately question whether the Yahwist's attention to the creation story was occasioned, and to some degree favored, by the theological or cultural climate in which he lived. If he did not have support from the received tradition in his bold linking of the Urgeschichte to the Heilsgeschichte, as von Rad maintains is the case,[20] then he may

---

[19] Genesis [124], pp. 27–30.

[20] Ibid., pp. 22–23. Though differing with von Rad in other respects, Noth agrees that the Vorbau of the primeval history goes back to the Yahwist, "who, through this contribution, invested his work with that theological breadth and depth which make it one of the most important components of the transmitted Pentateuch" (Ueberlieferungsgeschichte [117], p. 43).

have had support from his contemporary environment, and specifically from the royal cult of Jerusalem, in his project of historicizing the creation-faith.

Recent studies in the history of Israel's tradition have demanded a revision of the old view of a religious development traceable in the succesive Pentateuchal strata symbolized by J, E, D, and P. It is now recognized that these traditions, quite apart from the date of their final *literary* composition, represent parallel streams which have their source in the ancient formative period. Moreover, these four tributaries can be considered as essentially two great rivers: one which flowed through North Israel (that is, E and D) and the other through South Israel or Judah (that is, J and P). The split which emerged in the United Kingdom at the death of Solomon was not just political. It was fundamentally an ideological, or perhaps we should say a theological, cleavage which had very deep roots in differing understandings of the nature of Yahweh's covenant relation with Israel. If I may resort to a risky and obviously inadequate analogy, just as in the United States, there are two differing understandings of American history (one northern, and the other southern), so in ancient Israel there were two differing views of Yahweh's covenant with his people: one northern (E, D) and the other southern (J, P). Murray Newman has attempted to explain this ideological conflict, which erupted into revolution at the time of the death of Solomon, by tracing the two traditions back into the period before the settlement in Canaan, when controversy over the meaning of the covenant broke out at Kadesh-barnea.[21]

Now, when one looks at these two streams of tradition from the standpoint of our interest in the creation-faith, a very striking thing comes to light. Creation is a central theological concern in the southern tradition; indeed, the two creation stories with which the Bible opens come to us from the South—from P (Gen. 1:1—2:4a) and J (Gen. 2:4b—25). On the other hand, creation is at best peripheral in the two northern traditions,

---

[21] Murray L. Newman, Jr., *The People of the Covenant* [116].

E and D. The E epic begins with the call of Abraham (Gen. 15) and therefore is closely tied to Israel's *Heilsgeschichte*.[22] The same holds true for D. The introduction to the Deuteronomistic History (Josh. through II Kings) contains a passing reference to creation as the beginning of history:

> For ask now of the days that are past, which were before you, since the day that God created man upon the earth, and ask from one end of heaven to the other, whether such a great thing as this has ever happened or was ever heard of. Did any people ever hear the voice of a god speaking out of the midst of the fire, as you have heard, and still live? Or has any god ever attempted to go and take a nation for himself from the midst of another nation, by trials, by signs, by wonders, and by war, by a mighty hand and an outstretched arm, and by great terrors, according to all that Yahweh your God did for you in Egypt before your eyes?
>
> —DEUTERONOMY 4:32–34

But even this passage shows that the fulcrum of Deuteronomic theology is Israel's election manifested in the Exodus, and not the universal vista of the creation-faith. Moreover, this same theological accent is found in a prophetic work which is clearly and indisputably northern: the prophecy of Hosea. Not once does Hosea appeal to faith in Yahweh as creator of heaven and earth, even though he is constantly concerned with the agricultural blessings of fertility—"the grain, the wine, and the oil"—which Israelites had supposed were the gifts of Baal. Instead, he appeals to the sacred history (the Exodus, the wilderness sojourn, the gift of the land) and thus does not exceed the boundaries of the sacred history preserved in the northern (E) epic. The statement in Hosea 8:14 that "Israel has forgotten his Maker" refers, of course, to the formation of the community and thus interprets creation as an event of *Heilsgeschichte*.[23]

---

22 Attempts have been made to show that E elements are present in Gen. 1–11, but these have failed. One of the best attempts is that of Sigmund Mowinckel, *The Two Sources of the Predeuteronomic Primeval History (JE) in Gen. 1–11* [111].

23 There is no need to suppose that Hos. 8:14 introduces an idea later than Hosea; cf. James M. Ward, *Hosea* [153], pp. 144 f.

Admittedly, this apparent soft-pedaling of creation theology in the northern tradition may be only the result of the incompleteness of evidence. For we have to remember that northern traditions, after the fall of Samaria in 722 B.C., survived only in fragmentary form in the South, where they were used editorially to supplement and enrich the southern tradition. Yet, if northern tradition actually had stressed creation, it seems likely that southern traditionists would have made something of it—at least for the sake of supplementing and supporting southern creation theology, as was done elsewhere when parallel traditions were at hand.[24] In any case, this is the situation that we now find in the Old Testament: northern tradition, insofar as it is preserved in E, D, and Hosea, does not stress creation; on the other hand, southern tradition represented in J and P, to say nothing of the psalms which have survived from the Jerusalem cult, stress the importance of creation for Israel's faith. There is mounting evidence that, as R. E. Clements put it, "the Jerusalem cult in particular, with its own distinctive heritage, placed a quite exceptional emphasis upon the cosmic and supranational power of Yahweh, as the King of the Universe." [25] This being the case, we would expect that the creation-faith was especially at home in Jerusalem, where profound theological changes took place as a result of the rise of David as king.

IV

The reference to the "distinctive heritage" of the Jerusalem cult leads to a consideration of the royal covenant theology which developed in the South, in distinction from the Mosaic covenant theology which was probably perpetuated in the North. In recent years it has become increasingly clear that it is an oversimplification to speak of *the* covenant, as though

---

[24] E.g. the story of the making of the Sinai covenant is preserved in both J and E versions: Ex. 24:1–2, 9–11 [J]; 3–8 [E].

[25] *Prophecy and Covenant* [29], p. 20. See also Harvey H. Guthrie, Jr. (*Israel's Sacred Songs* [69], Chap. 2), who stresses that under David's leadership "Israel entered the cosmos" and that in Jerusalem worship was defined by the theme of "God as cosmic king."

this term were an umbrella covering the whole Old Testament. At least *two* covenant traditions were current during the period of the divided monarchy, both of which may reach far back into Israel's history. These covenant traditions conceive the relation between God and Israel in terms of analogies drawn from political and social experience, that is, the pacts or treaties made between individuals or between groups.[26] The first covenant type is illustrated in ancient Hittite treaties between the great king and his vassal: the so-called suzerainty treaty. Characteristically it begins with a historical prologue which summarizes the king's deeds of benevolence, it announces stipulations which the vassal is to accept obediently, and it invokes sanctions of blessing or cursing to uphold the covenant. In this type of covenant there is a conditional or contingent element. *The covenant recipient is bound in obligation* to the covenant maker, who surrenders his freedom only to the extent that he pledges not to use his power arbitrarily. This covenant (or treaty) remains in force as long as the vassal obeys, motivated by gratitude for what the king had done on his behalf. Typologically, it is like the Mosaic covenant presupposed in the E stratum of Exodus 19–24.

> You have seen what I did to the Egyptians, and how I bore you on eagles' wings and brought you to myself. Now therefore, if you will obey my voice and keep my covenant, you shall be my own possession among all peoples; for all the earth is mine, and you shall be to me a kingdom of priests and a holy nation.
>
> —Exodus 19:4–6a [E]

The second type of covenant is one in which *the covenant maker binds himself* by an oath, without prescribing conditions for the continuance of the relationship. Typologically, this treaty is like the patriarchal covenant-tradition which circulated apparently in the region of Hebron where the Abra-

---

26 In this connection see especially the article "Covenant" by George E. Mendenhall, *The Interpreter's Dictionary of the Bible* [104], also his pioneering monograph, *Law and Covenant in Israel and the Ancient Near East* [103].

ham stories were at home. For instance, in the archaic covenant ceremony described in the J passage in Genesis 15:7–21, the deity passes through the bloody corridor between the sacrificed birds and animals and thereby submits to the oath (cf. Jer. 34:18–19!). The deity binds himself to the covenant promise, without imposing any conditions upon Abraham, the recipient, who at this time is in a *tardemah,* a deep sleep (15:12). Similarly, the P version of the Abrahamic covenant found in Genesis 17 is unilateral. It is based solely upon the word of *'El Shaddai* ("God Almighty"), without any conditions—for circumcision is here understood as the external sign of membership in the covenant community, not the conditional basis of the covenant. This covenant is described as a *berith 'olam,* an "everlasting covenant" (17:7).

How these two covenant traditions came to be blended in Israelite tradition is a problem which cannot occupy us here. For our purpose it is important to notice that in Jerusalem there developed a *berith 'olam* ("everlasting covenant") theology and that this covenant theology was peculiarly interested in creation. The theology of the Davidic covenant is set forth in II Samuel 7, a passage which undoubtedly rests on tradition going back to the Davidic court circle.[27] Here we read that Yahweh enters into a special relationship with Israel *through* the Davidic king who reigns in Jerusalem. He promises unconditionally to establish the Davidic house *forever ('ad 'olam),* that is, in perpetuity (vss. 13, 16). He elects the reigning Davidic king to be his adopted son: "I will be his father, and he shall be my son" (vs. 14; cf. Ps. 2:7). And he gives assurance that, regardless of the performance of successors on the throne, he will not withdraw his steadfast love *(ḥesed)* from the king. Here is a covenant which removes elements of contingency and provides a divine *guarantee* of order, stability, security. The

---

[27] It is maintained that in the message of the prophet Nathan (vss. 11b and 16) are old elements which probably go back to the time of David and that the prophetic oracle has been expanded with later traditions. See, for instance, H. J. Kraus, *Worship in Israel* [93], pp. 179–81, and especially the definitive study by Leonhard Rost, *Die Ueberlieferung von der Thronnachfolge Davids* [134], pp. 47 ff.

same idea is expressed in the so-called "Last Words of David," which probably come from David himself:

> Yea, does not my house stand so with God?
> For he has made with me an everlasting covenant,
> ordered in all things and secure.
> For will he not cause to prosper
> all my help and my desire?
>
> —II SAMUEL 23:5

A theology concerned with stressing the perpetuity of the Davidic dynasty in the face of the disruptive forces that threatened it could have appealed profitably to the ancient Near Eastern creation-faith, which, as we have seen, was governed by fundamentally the same concern: order, security, stability. It is significant that in the Near Eastern cults the king—whether regarded as divine as in Egyptian religion or the representative or vicegerent of the god as in Babylonian—played a key role. Being the mediator through whom the divine order of creation flowed out into society, he was the administrator of "justice" (order) and the champion of the state against enemy threats from the outside. And because of the king's special relation to the divine realm, he exercised an important cultic role in the temple, which was variously believed to be built on the primeval hill, or at the center (navel) of the earth, where creation emerged out of chaos.[28] If Israel was to become "like all the nations" in having a king (I Sam. 8:4–22), the theology of kingship would probably be appropriated too, along with the political centralization of power. To be sure, creation theology when linked with Davidic covenant theology would be radically transformed. No longer would creation belong in the sphere of nature, where man was caught up annually in the

---

28 P. Ricoeur [132] maintains that the Babylonian creation mythology leads ultimately to a theology of war, according to which political enemies are identified with "the powers that the god has vanquished and continues to vanquish in the drama of creation." Thus the king's participation in the cult is the bond that ties the political to the cosmic. "Through the mediation of the king," he writes, "the drama of creation becomes significant for the whole history of mankind, and particularly for all of that aspect of human life which is characterized by combat."

dramatic conflict between cosmos and chaos, and thus part of the *cyclical* divine process which sustains the world. Rather, it would become part of a historical religion whose center, according to the Jerusalem court, was Yahweh's action in raising up David to be king and in choosing Jerusalem as the central sanctuary for Israel, a once-for-all event which inaugurated a new historical epoch. What the Davidic covenant interpreters wanted to say was that this event in its double aspect—the choice of David as king and the choice of Zion as Yahweh's abode—was ordained by the God who made heaven and earth, the God whose unconditional promise stands *forever*.

It is hardly accidental, then, that one of the earliest references to Yahweh as creator is found in the narrative about Solomon's celebration of the Feast of Tabernacles, the fall pilgrimage festival. In the ancient prayer, which may well come from Solomon's time, it is said that "Yahweh has set the sun in the heavens" and that Solomon has built Yahweh "an exalted house" for him to dwell in forever.

> Then Solomon said:
> "Yahweh has set the sun in the heavens,
>   but has said that he would dwell in thick darkness.
> I have built thee an exalted house,
>   a place for thee to dwell in for ever."
> —I Kings 8:12–13 [29]

The assumption of this passage is probably the ancient view that the Jerusalem temple was a microcosm of the macrocosm, an earthly replica of the heavenly temple—a view which enabled Israel to believe that Yahweh was truly present in Mount Zion and at the same time the transcendent God of the heavens.[30] Since the Jerusalem cult was profoundly influenced by

---

[29] The first line of the prayer is restored according to the Greek (Septuagint).

[30] G. E. Wright points out that this view, evidenced in Egypt and elsewhere, prevailed in the case of Canaanite temples and the temple of Solomon; see his and others' articles in *The Biblical Archaeologist Reader* [165], pp. 145–200. The theological significance of this view for the Jerusalem temple has been discussed by R. E. Clements, *God and Temple* [30], Chap. 5.

this *vertical* correspondence between the celestial and the terrestrial,[31] it manifested a peculiar interest in the cosmic rule of the God who was worshiped in the earthly temple. One evidence of this was the installation of "the molten sea" in the temple of Solomon (I Kings 7:23–26), a piece of cultic equipment which doubtless signified the cosmic sea, the *Tehom*, that is, the waters under the earth which are the source of fertility (cf. Gen. 49:25: "blessings of the deep [*tehom*] that couches beneath").[32] Furthermore the "holy mountain" upon which the temple stood could be compared to the sacred mountain in the far north, the divine abode:

> His holy mountain, beautiful in elevation,
>   is the joy of all the earth,
> Mount Zion, in the far north,
>   the city of the great King.
> Within her citadels God
>   has shown himself a sure defense.
>   —PSALM 48:2–3

Since it was believed that God dwells in the earthly counterpart of his heavenly abode, it could be said that "the city of our God" is established forever (vs. 8). In other words, the stability of Zion is guaranteed by the stability of the cosmos.

It is significant, too, that Solomon's dedicatory prayer, referred to above, was made in connection with the autumnal festival: the Feast of Tabernacles or the New Year celebration. On this occasion, as we shall see more fully in the next chapter, Yahweh was praised as the king of the cosmos in a ceremony in which the Davidic king, his vicegerent, played a major part. Doubtless this festival provided the cultic context for blending creation motifs of the ancient world—mythological elements not only from Canaan but also from Mesopotamia and even Egypt—with the themes composing Israel's sacred history.[33]

---

[31] See especially Mircea Eliade's discussion of "celestial archetypes," *Cosmos and History* [44], pp. 6 ff.

[32] Cf. Albright, *Archaeology and the Religion of Israel* [8], pp. 148 ff.

[33] Cf. R. E. Clements, *God and Temple* [30], pp. 69–70.

Also, in Psalm 78 we find that the belief in Yahweh's cosmic power is matched by the belief that he dwells in Mount Zion. This psalm recapitulates Israel's sacred history from the time of the Exodus but, surprisingly, it comes to a climax with the announcement that Yahweh has rejected North Israel and has chosen Judah. Here we find that the stability of the cosmos is the basis of the security of Zion and the perpetuity of the Davidic dynasty:

> He built his sanctuary like the high heavens,
>   like the earth, which he has founded for ever.
> He chose David his servant,
>   and took him from the sheepfolds;
> from tending the ewes that had young he brought him
>   to be the shepherd of Jacob his people,
>   of Israel his inheritance.
>
> —PSALM 78:69–71

Even more impressive testimony to the place of creation-faith in the royal cult of Jerusalem is found in Psalm 89, a community lament which is based on Davidic theology. It consists of three parts: a song to Yahweh who has made a covenant with David and his house (vss. 1–37); a lament prompted by the apparent violation of that covenant (vss. 38–45); and a fervent petition for Yahweh to remember his steadfast love of old and to remove the national distress (vss. 46–52). The psalm must be pre-exilic, for it reflects a time when a Davidic king was still reigning in Jerusalem.[34] It presupposes the fundamental tenet of Davidic covenant theology: the covenant rests upon Yahweh's oath.

> Thou hast said, "I have made a covenant with my chosen one,
>   I have sworn to David my servant:
> 'I will establish your descendants for ever,
>   and build your throne for all generations.' "
>
> —PSALM 89:3–4

Accordingly, the psalmist begins by extolling Yahweh's ḥesed,

---

[34] See O. Eissfeldt, "The Promises of Grace to David" [43].

which is established forever, his faithfulness, which is firm as the heavens (vs. 2). And the motif of the everlasting stability of the Davidic throne leads smoothly into a hymn praising Yahweh's supremacy as creator in the Heavenly Council, and, specifically, his triumph over the chaos monster, here named Rahab.[35]

> Let the heavens praise thy wonders, O Yahweh,
> thy faithfulness in the assembly of the holy ones!
> For who in the skies can be compared to Yahweh?
> Who among the heavenly beings is like Yahweh,
> a God feared in the council of the holy ones,
> great and terrible above all that are round about him?
> O Yahweh God of hosts,
> who is mighty as thou art, O Yahweh,
> with thy faithfulness round about thee?
>
> Thou dost rule the raging of the sea;
> when its waves rise, thou stillest them.
> Thou didst crush Rahab like a carcass,
> thou didst scatter thy enemies with thy mighty arm.
> The heavens are thine, the earth also is thine;
> the world and all that is in it, thou hast founded them.
> —PSALM 89:5–11

Here Yahweh's power in the creation is related theologically to his covenant with David. Yahweh has established, and he will maintain, order, for "righteousness and justice" are the foundation of his throne. The Davidic king, standing in this strength, will not be overpowered by any foes; indeed, his world dominion is described in language which may echo creation mythology:

> "I will set his hand on the sea
> and his right hand on the rivers."
> —PSALM 89:25

---

[35] See the discussion of this psalm by Samuel Terrien, in "Creation, Cultus, and Faith in the Psalter" [146], especially pp. 119–21. He stresses that the myth of the fight with the chaos monster is here "a merely stylistic device, with a possible overtone of poetic personification of the numinous," and that the poet's intention is "to establish hymnically the omnipotence of the Lord of history."

Thus powerful support is given to the certainty that the Davidic dynasty is stable and secure.

> "His line shall endure for ever,
>   his throne as long as the sun before me.
> Like the moon it shall be established for ever;
>   it shall stand firm while the skies endure."
>   —PSALM 89:36–37

To be sure, this certainty, which is grounded not only in Yahweh's covenant oath but also in his faithfulness and might as creator, throws into sharp relief the bitter distress of the present when historical chaos prevails and intensifies the fervency of prayer for deliverance.

V

The Jerusalem cult, then, was undoubtedly a crucible for the fusion of the creation-faith with the faith based upon Israel's sacred history, now understood to culminate with the election of David and the election of Zion, as Psalm 78 shows. In view of this, it should not be surprising that the two accounts of creation with which the Bible begins, that of P and that of J, were composed in the theological atmosphere of Jerusalem. Both P and J are concerned to emphasize the cosmic rule of Yahweh, whose power in creation undergirds and supports the course of Israel's sacred history. Both insist that Yahweh's covenant is the foundation of history's meaning and the assurance of the continuity of his purpose. The biblical story of the Flood, unlike the Babylonian parallel which expresses divine caprice, intends to portray a meaningful event (Yahweh's judgment upon human sin). In the Yahwist version it concludes with Yahweh's pledge: "While the earth remains, seedtime and harvest, cold and heat, summer and winter, day and night, shall not cease" (Gen. 8:22). Thus the regularities of nature, which modern men have rationalized into "laws," are at bottom expressions of the faithfulness of God upon which men rely. According to the P version, the Flood was a new outbreak of the waters of chaos, a cosmic catastrophe which threatened to return the earth to its precreation condition. But God caused a wind to blow over the earth, and the waters subsided (Gen. 8:1), whereupon he established an "everlasting covenant" (Gen. 9:16) signified by the rainbow. The covenant between him and the earth was his unconditional promise, guaranteed solely by his word (oath), that never again would the waters of chaos threaten human history with profound disorder. The new beginning was essentially a re-creation.[36]

The Jerusalem cult was undoubtedly influenced by other circles within which creation was a major concern. First of all, it is very likely, as a number of scholars have argued, that when David captured Jerusalem by a surprise stratagem (II Sam. 5:6–10), he became the heir of political and theological traditions which were deeply established in the former Jebusite stronghold.[37] For centuries before David, Jerusalem had been one of the city-states of Palestine, though subordinate in importance to major city-states like Shechem, Megiddo, or Bethshean. Jebusite Jerusalem was governed by a monarchy, as we know from Joshua 10:1–27, which mentions the leadership of a king named Adonizedek. And these pre-Davidic kings played an important role in the cult, to judge from the mention of the priest-king Melchizedek in Genesis 14 (cf. Ps. 110:4), a chapter which stands apart from the major traditions of the Pentateuch. Indeed, if we may rely on this chapter as a source which preserves pre-Davidic tradition, it appears that in pre-Israelite, Jebusite Jerusalem men worshiped 'Elyon, or 'El 'Elyon ("God Most High") under the epithet "maker [qoneh] of heaven and earth" (Gen. 14:19). This epithet, which also

---

36 This point is made by Herbert G. May in his article, "Some Cosmic Connotations of *Mayim Rabbîm*, 'Many Waters'" [100]. He observes (p. 14, n. 19) that just as Marduk used the wind to conquer Tiamat, so during the Flood "when the waters had once more ruled and re-creation became necessary," God sent a wind to make them subside. He also calls attention to the "re-creation terminology" in Gen. 9:1–2.

37 See, for instance, Aubrey Johnson, *Sacral Kingship in Ancient Israel* [85], pp. 27–46; this position is also taken by Harvey Guthrie [69], pp. 71–74.

occurs in other Canaanite texts, was—as Frank Cross puts it—
"a liturgical sobriquet, originating in the cult of Canaanite
'*El*." [38] Moreover, it is possible to go a step further. If in Canaanite mythology El was revered as creator, while Baal's conflict with Sea and River was connected with the recurring
rhythms of nature (see above, pp. 24–26), Jerusalem may have
been a place where the worship of El, "the creator of creatures," was fused with the Baal ideology of the Canaanite New
Year festival.[39] In any case, it is significant that, according to
the story in Genesis 14, Abram identifies El Elyon with *Yahweh,* "maker of heaven and earth" (vs. 22)—a bold identification which seems to indicate that under David, Israel captured
not only a city but also a creation theology.

Genesis 14, therefore, provides striking evidence of the mediation of Canaanite theological motifs to Israel via the Jebusite cult. The importance of this influence upon the Jerusalem cult of David is further strengthened if H. H. Rowley is
correct in saying that David adopted the Zadokite priesthood
from the former Jebusite city and promised it an everlasting
priesthood (cf. Ps. 110:4).[40] Apparently David initially sought
the support of both Abiathar, whose line was traced back to
the high priests of the former Tribal Confederacy, and Zadok,
who represented the priestly line of pre-Davidic Jerusalem. In
this way he tried to pacify the conservative elements of the Israelite tribes and at the same time to court the favor of the
Jebusites of Jerusalem. But the difficulty of mixing native Israelite tradition with Canaanite tradition is perhaps drama-
tized in the story of the contest between Adonijah and Solomon for the Davidic throne. In this contest Abiathar, who
with backing from David's companions of his early career sup-

---

[38] See his essay on patriarchal religion [34], p. 244.

[39] Cf. J. Gray, *The Legacy of Canaan* [66], p. 33. It should be emphasized, however, that the Jebusite cult was not the source of creation motifs
but only influenced the expression of what was already present in Israelite
tradition. On this point see the remarks of Cross in "The Divine Warrior" [35], p. 24, n. 23.

[40] See the essay by H. H. Rowley, "Melchizedek and Zadok (Gen. 14 and
Ps. 110)" [136]; also "Zadok and Nehushtan" [135].

ported Adonijah, was exiled, and Zadok, who with backing from the Jerusalem court supported Solomon, became the chief priest of the Jerusalem temple (I Kings 1 and 2).

From another direction, namely, from Israel's wisdom movement, came influences which emphasized the creation-faith and reinterpreted the old chaos mythology. The tradition that Solomon was the patron of wisdom must be taken seriously. At a very early period in the monarchy, and probably under the sponsorship of Solomon, wisdom reflections modified and enriched the Israelite faith. Israel's sages drew upon the mythopoeic imagery of the ancient Near East not only to magnify God's power by extolling his first and most marvelous work but also to reflect upon the wonderful order and regularity in the universe. Even as late as the book of Job (perhaps around the year 600 B.C.) a poet could draw upon the old Canaanite myth of Baal's triumph over "Leviathan the Primaeval Serpent . . . the Crooked Serpent, the Close-coiling One of Seven Heads," though definitely connecting the imagery with the power of the Creator:

"He stretches out the north over the void,
and hangs the earth upon nothing.
He binds up the waters in his thick clouds,
and the cloud is not rent under them.
He covers the face of the moon,
and spreads over it his cloud.
He has described a circle upon the face of the waters
at the boundary between light and darkness.
The pillars of heaven tremble,
and are astounded at his rebuke.
By his power he stilled the sea;
by his understanding he smote Rahab.
By his wind the heavens were made fair;
his hand pierced the fleeing serpent.
Lo, these are but the outskirts of his ways;
and how small a whisper do we hear of him!
But the thunder of his power who can understand?"
—Job 26:7–14

(See also Ps. 74:12–17, perhaps from about the same period, where the Creator is praised for "breaking the heads of the dragons on the waters," for "crushing the heads of Leviathan.")

In another passage from the book of Job, the tempestuous spirit of Job is quieted by the reminder that he, a creature, was not present when the Creator, like an architect building a house, constructed the universe by marking off the boundaries, sinking the foundations of the earth, and laying the corner-stone, and when, beholding this marvelous structure, "the morning stars sang together, and all the sons of God shouted for joy" (Job 38:4–7).[41] Job is then reminded of how the Creator sheltered his cosmic construction from the dangers of chaos:

> ". . . who shut in the sea with doors,
>   when it burst forth from the womb;
> when I made clouds its garment,
>   and thick darkness its swaddling band,
> and prescribed bounds for it,
>   and set bars and doors,
> and said, 'Thus far shall you come, and no farther,
>   and here shall your proud waves be stayed'?"
>   —Job 38:8–11

Similarly the composer of Psalm 104 joyfully affirms that men live in a universe ordered by wisdom (see vs. 24: "In wisdom hast thou made them all"), where every creature has its proper place and function in the whole scheme. Thanks to the influence of Israel's wisdom movement, it could be affirmed that at the time of the creation Yahweh set bounds which the waters of chaos should not pass and even converted them to beneficial use.

> Thou didst set the earth on its foundations,
>   so that it should never be shaken.
> Thou didst cover it with the deep [tehom] as with a garment;
>   the waters stood above the mountains.

---

[41] Edmund Jacob (*Theology of the Old Testament* [81], pp. 136 f.) stresses that the wisdom metaphor of the architect is implicit in the Priestly story in Gen. 1.

At thy rebuke they fled;
  at the sound of thy thunder they took to flight.
The mountains rose, the valleys sank down
  to the place which thou didst appoint for them.
Thou didst set a bound which they should not pass,
  so that they might not again cover the earth.
                                    —PSALM 104:5–9

As we shall see in the next chapter, the affinities between Psalm 104 and the Priestly creation story in Genesis 1 are so close that both must reflect the liturgical practice of the Jerusalem temple. In view of the parallels between Psalm 104 and the Egyptian "Hymn to the Sun," to which attention has already been called, it is apparent that wisdom motifs influenced the Jerusalem cult by way of Israel's sages. Israel's wise men wanted to say with their own accent that the Creator has established order in the world and that he maintains that order against any threat of chaos.

The most sophisticated use of the chaos motif in Israel's wisdom literature is found in Proverbs 8. According to this passage, wisdom was older than the primeval waters of chaos, and attended Yahweh in the successive works of creation, including his assigning a limit to the unruly waters of chaos (cf. Ps. 104:9).

When he established the heavens, I was there,
  when he drew a circle on the face of the deep,
when he made firm the skies above,
  when he established the fountains of the deep,
when he assigned to the sea its limit,
  so that the waters might not transgress his command,
when he marked out the foundations of the earth,
  then I was beside him, like a master workman;
and I was daily his delight,
  rejoicing before him always,
rejoicing in his inhabited world,
  and delighting in the sons of men.
                                    —PROVERBS 8:27–31

Without entering into the question of the date of this passage in the wisdom tradition or the disputed question of the word here translated as "a master workman" (vs. 30),[42] it is evident that the poem belongs in a circle of sages who over the generations refined mythological ideas of creation and made them serviceable to Israel's faith.[43]

VI

All of this points to the conclusion that the division within Israel which occurred after the death of Solomon had far deeper theological roots than many of us have realized. Fundamentally two different conceptions of Israel's covenant relation with God were at stake. In the North there was a far greater emphasis upon the call to covenant obedience and the fateful choice which Israel had to make when Yahweh was setting before his people the alternatives of life or death. It is not surprising that in this theological atmosphere, which preserved the freedom of the old Tribal Confederacy, no single dynasty was able to maintain itself throughout the history of the northern kingdom. So seriously was the contingent nature of the covenant taken in the North that prophets who spoke there— Amos and Hosea—boldly drew from Israel's covenant disobedience the inevitable consequence: the end has come upon Israel.

In contrast, the southern covenant tradition reduced the element of historical contingency to a minimum by stressing the unconditional oath which Yahweh swore to David and by appealing to Yahweh's power as creator and sovereign of the universe. The God who in the beginning pushed back the waters of chaos continues to maintain order and to preserve the continuity of the Davidic dynasty. It has often been observed that this theology helped to maintain political stability in Judah, where a single dynasty ruled from David to the fall of the nation. The great prophet Isaiah, whose message was keyed to

---

[42] See R. B. Y. Scott, *Proverbs and Ecclesiastes* [140], pp. 69–73; also his article "Wisdom in Creation: the *'āmōn* of Proverbs viii 30" [141].

[43] See T. H. Gaster, "Cosmogony" [58], especially pp. 705–6.

this covenant theology, preached that God's judgment would purge Jerusalem and restore it as at the beginning, that a remnant would be preserved to be the nucleus of a New Jerusalem, and that a "messianic" king would spring from the stem of Jesse to rule with wisdom and righteousness.

One of the contributions of George Mendenhall's form-critical study of the legal form known as the "covenant" (referred to above, pp. 60–63) is that we are enabled to understand more clearly how these "two opposing concepts of religion" coexisted in uneasy tension in the biblical period, beginning with the time of the monarchy when the theological conflict between them broke out. "On the one hand," he writes, referring to the suzerainty covenant type, "there is the emphasis on the experience of the past as the foundation of obligation, the emphasis upon direct responsibility to God, upon *freedom and self-determination*—all of which, degenerating, leads to chaos." [44] This is the essential emphasis of the Mosaic covenant in which, as we have seen, the creation-faith had a secondary place. "On the other hand," Mendenhall writes, referring to the Davidic covenant, there is "the emphasis upon *stability and continuity,* the attempt to reduce the actions of God to a readily communicable and comprehensible system, the preservation of a particular cultural pattern and the establishment of authority to hold in check the unpredictable and disruptive tendencies of undisciplined humanity—all of which may also degenerate and lead to stagnation and satisfaction with the status quo, even if it must be maintained by sheer force." His concluding remark is most significant for our study: *"It may also lead to myth—by identifying itself with the divine power which defeats the powers of chaos."* [45] As we have seen, a covenant theology of this type was especially hospitable to creation motifs of ancient Near Eastern religions which stressed the maintenance of stability and order in the face of the chaotic threats of historical change and contingency.

Cannot these two theological traditions be traced into our

---

[44] *Law and Covenant* [103], p. 50.
[45] *Ibid.,* p. 50. All italics are mine.

own time? In our situation we know, perhaps too well, the contingency of human history, the terrible possibilities of human
freedom, the awful prospect of "the eve of destruction." God
has summoned us in the depth of our historical existence to
decide who we are, and whom we will serve; and the alternatives are set before us: life and death, good and evil, blessing
and curse. We can scarcely bear to consider the terrible conse-
quences which could follow man's decision. Jeremiah's vision
of the return of chaos speaks to us with haunting realism.

> I looked on the earth, and lo, it was waste and void;
>   and to the heavens, and they had no light.
>   —JEREMIAH 4:23

And there are times when the words of a prophet like Amos
ring out the inevitable conclusion: the end has come upon my
people!

But there is also another theological tradition which we
need to know. It witnesses more to the promises of grace which
God has made with men unconditionally, through him who is
greater than David. It speaks of the Creator's faithfulness
which underlies all things, providing a basis for ultimate meaning in human history which finally cannot be destroyed by any
of the unruly powers of chaos. The author of Psalm 46, one of
the great hymns of Zion, speaks out of this theological understanding. He employs the old cosmological imagery about the
founding of the earth upon the abyss, the waters of chaos; but
he transforms the imagery to praise the God who is Lord of
history.

> God is our refuge and strength,
>   a very present help in trouble.
> Therefore we will not fear though the earth should change,
>   though the mountains shake in the heart of the sea;
>   though its waters roar and foam,
>   though the mountains tremble with its tumult.
>   —PSALM 46:1-3

The picture of the raging of the chaotic powers of creation
fades into the picture of the raging of the nations against

Mount Zion, and this in turn prepares for the final word of
the One whose will is sovereign over the tumult of history:

> "Be still, and know that I am God.
> I am exalted among the nations,
> I am exalted in the earth!"
> —PSALM 46:10

It is this psalm which, transposed by Luther into a Christian
key, has become the Church's great victory hymn:

> A Mighty Fortress is our God,
> a Bulwark never failing;
> Our helper He amid the flood,
> of mortal ills prevailing.

CHAPTER

3

Creation and Worship

SOME YEARS AGO Bishop Hanns Lilje, in answer to a question about the condition of the Church in East Germany, portrayed to a conference of American students a great *Kirchentag* held in Leipzig, to which city some six hundred thousand people had gathered for discussion, fellowship, and worship. The great gathering took place in the very shadow of a Communist building, at the top of which was the Red Star. In front of the building was a statue of Stalin, a detail which dates this story well before the time when Stalin was "demythologized." "Right under Stalin's nose," as the bishop whimsically put it, a sermon was preached on the opening words of the Twenty-fourth Psalm:

> The earth is the Lord's and the fulness thereof,
>   the world and those who dwell therein;
> for he has founded it upon the seas,
>   and established it upon the rivers.
> —PSALM 24:1–2

One would think that the text, with its affirmation that God established the earth upon waters, would have been completely irrelevant in the sophisticated twentieth century, when any grammar school student knows that the earth orbits in space.

78

The statement in verse 2 that God founded the earth upon the "seas" (yammim), established it upon the "rivers" (neharoth), clearly reflects the ancient view of the earth as an island suspended over the primeval ocean and faintly echoes the myth of the divine victory over the hostile powers of chaos, explicitly named Sea (Yam) and River (Nahar) in Canaanite mythological texts (see above, pp. 24 ff.). But in that situation of worship the intention of the text was probably more evident than in the usual arguments about science and religion. For the creation-faith's insistence that the earth belongs to God is a challenge to man's self-understanding. Doctrinaire communism has to deny the biblical meaning of creation, not just for the spurious reason that it conflicts with a scientific world-view but for the deeper reason that it is existentially unacceptable to modern man. Pious people may be allowed to say that "heaven" belongs to the Lord; but one thing is clear to this-worldly "realists" for whom scientific knowledge is power: the earth belongs to man and is subject to his control.[1]

I

The setting of the creation-faith within worship is clearly evident in Psalm 24, which undoubtedly was once used in connection with a processional bearing of the Ark into Jerusalem during a great pilgrimage festival celebrating Yahweh's kingship. The psalm has three sections: an introit which announces that Yahweh is creator (vss. 1–2), an "entrance Torah" in question-and-answer form (vss. 3–6) like the one in Psalm 15, and finally an "entrance liturgy" which was sung antiphonally in the presence of the Ark, the throne-seat of "Yahweh of hosts" (cf. I Sam. 4:4; II Sam. 6:2), as the company of worshipers stood before the gates of Jerusalem.[2] In this liturgical setting

---

1 Elements of this chapter are taken from my article "The Earth is the Lord's: An Essay on the Biblical Doctrine of Creation" [12].

2 See Hans-Joachim Kraus, Worship in Israel [93], pp. 208–18, for an attempt to delineate the structure of the festival cult at Jerusalem, with

the function of creation language is to give the *ground* for praising God. The worshiping community confesses that the earth, and all the creatures it contains, belong solely to the Yahweh, *for* he is creator and king. His power upholds the world and his purpose gives meaning to existence. Thus in the book of Psalms the affirmation that God is the creator is a *Venite*, a call to worship.

> O come, let us sing to Yahweh;
>> let us make a joyful noise to the rock of our salvation!
> Let us come into his presence with thanksgiving;
>> let us make a joyful noise to him with songs of praise!
> For Yahweh is a great God,
>> and a great King above all gods.
> In his hand are the depths of the earth;
>> the heights of the mountains are his also.
> The sea is his, for he made it;
>> for his hands formed the dry land.
>
> —PSALM 95:1-5

To the psalmist the greatness of Yahweh is shown in the fact that even the extremities of the world—from the heights of the mountains (in popular thought the abode of the gods) to the depths of the earth (the realm of the powers of darkness and death)—are under his control (cf. Amos 9:2-3; Ps. 139:7-12). The sea and the dry land, the lofty mountains and the abysses of the earth are *his*, not because he extended his domain to include them, like a king who enlarges his empire, but because he made them and they were his from the first.

In the succeeding lines of Psalm 95 the *Venite* is repeated, though this time it is grounded upon the creation of Israel.

> O come, let us worship and bow down,
>> let us kneel before Yahweh, our Maker!
> For he is our God,
>> and we are the people of his pasture,
>> and the sheep of his hand.
>
> —PSALM 95:6-7

---

special reference to Ps. 24. The "entrance-Torah" included the question of the right to enter (24:3), the declaration by the priests of the laws binding upon the people (vss. 4–5), and the response of the pilgrims (vs. 6).

Here the people of God are described under the image of the shepherd and his flock (cf. John 10). Creation implies *belonging to God* on the analogy of the sheep who are constituted as a flock by belonging to their shepherd. Israel affirms that Yahweh is "our Maker," the One who created a people *ex nihilo*, and therefore he is *our* God and we are *his* people (see Ps. 100:3, where the same affirmation is made). To believe in God the creator is to acknowledge that he is Lord absolutely.

Back in the 1920's, when a storm of controversy broke out over the doctrine of evolution, men passionately took sides in the "science versus religion" battle, some attempting to demonstrate that the biblical doctrine of creation is good science and others rejecting it as bad science. Now that the smoke of battle has lifted, we can see more clearly what the real issue is. The conflict does not lie fundamentally in the realm of scientific hypothesis about *how* the universe began or *how* man evolved. That false determination of the battlefront resulted from a failure to understand the intention of Israel's language of worship. Rather, the announcement that God is the creator primarily concerns the source and basis of life's meaning. Negatively, it rebukes the notion that the world is at man's disposal—susceptible to the meaning he imposes and subject to the purposes he devises. The earth is not man's, it is the Lord's; hence the meaning of man's life is not derived from the world. And, positively, the doctrine evokes in man an understanding of who he really is: a transient and contingent being who, together with all that exists, is dependent upon the God who alone is Lord. Man's life on earth derives its meaning from relationship to the God whose creative purpose has initiated the whole historical drama.

More and more we are coming to realize that the word *creation* belongs to a language which has a vocabulary and syntax of its own, a theological language whose affirmations should not be confused with statements made in the context of scientific language.[3] The creation-faith has to do with the meaning

---

3 In *The Logic of Self-involvement* [48] Donald Evans discusses the function of theological language about creation from the standpoint of modern philosophy of language.

of man's life—not only the meaning of *my* life in the world
here and now but the meaning of the whole historical process
which unfolds between the horizons of beginning and end.
Therefore theologians and scientists are coming to admit that
they may not be talking about the same thing when each
speaks of "creation" or "the beginning." In fact, a British scientist, Reginald O. Kapp, is reported to have advised his scientific colleagues to avoid using the theological word *creation*
and thereby to avoid semantic confusion.[4]

Considering the special character of the biblical language,
Claus Westermann is justified in suggesting that to understand
the creation stories at the beginning of the Bible we ought to
divest our minds of scientific and philosophical preconceptions
and to begin with the psalms which praise God as the creator.
"Praise of God, the Creator," he writes, "does not presuppose
the creation story, but quite the reverse: praise of God is the
source and presupposition of the creation story. The present
narrative is, in fact, a developed and expanded confession of
faith in God as Creator." [5] If I understand this statement cor-
rectly, Westermann is not suggesting that we start from a position in worship which is detached from Israel's sacred history
(Heilsgeschichte); rather, he is saying, the psalms of Israel help
us to understand that the story of creation is told *confessionally,* that is, to express faith in God, and not to engage in prescientific, prephilosophical reflections about nature. In other
words, the story of creation is a theological exposition of God's
redemptive activity, which is the ground of Israel's praise.

Certainly this is the case with the Priestly story of creation
with which the Bible opens. In its present *position,* of course,
this creation account is the opening of the whole historical
drama and accordingly is the prelude to the story of God's
special dealings with his people Israel, represented by Abra-

---

4 Cited by Carl Michalson, *The Rationality of Faith* [105], p. 47. In his
discussion of creation (pp. 42–48) this theologian pushes provocatively to
the extreme of saying that creation deals *only* with history and has no
application to the sphere of "nature" at all.

5 Claus Westermann, *A Thousand Years and a Day: Our Time in the
Old Testament* [156], p. 3.

ham. However, the *form* of the story suggests that it was shaped
by liturgical usage over a period of many generations, perhaps
in connection with one of the great pilgrimage festivals of
Israel, and thus it is told confessionally, to glorify the God of
Israel. This is the way the French scholar Paul Humbert wants
us to read the story. After comparing the close similarities between Genesis 1 and Psalm 104 (see the comparison below,
pp. 91–93) he concludes that both are *liturgical* texts associated
with the Israelite New Year festival—the fall harvest festival
known as the Feast of Tabernacles. In this respect Humbert
has taken a step which Gunkel did not think of taking. Gunkel had pointed out that Genesis 1 echoes motifs from the
Babylonian creation story, which was designed to be read on
the occasion of the *akitu* (New Year) festival; but he did not
consider Genesis 1 to be a *Festlegende* or cultic text designed
for use at the Israelite New Year festival. Humbert, however,
suggests that the Genesis story is structured in a seven-day
scheme, not to accommodate to an ordinary week but to reflect the *festal week,* the seven days of the Feast of Tabernacles
with which the New Year begins.[6]

Later on we shall return to the question of the New Year
feast, especially to the so-called "Enthronement Psalms" which
acclaim Yahweh as king of the universe. Quite apart from the
question as to whether Genesis 1, on the analogy of the Babylonian creation story, is a festal legend, there should be general
agreement on the fundamental point: the Priestly account of
creation, like the creation psalms of the Psalter, is a sublime
expression of Israel's praise. The creation story is most at home
in a setting of worship.

II

This leads to an important point. When the creation-faith is
interpreted within the context of worship there is a tendency
to shift the accent from creation as the event in the beginning

6 Paul Humbert, "La relation de Genèse 1 et du Psaume 104 avec la
liturgie du Nouvel-An israélite" [78].

to a relationship in the present, from the initiating act of the Creator to the creature's dependence upon the Creator. Here the vertical dimension (the relationship between God and man) is more important than the horizontal one (the movement of events from beginning to end). An excellent illustration is found at the beginning of Augustine's *Confessions,* where he utters the prayer: "O Lord, thou hast made us for thyself and our hearts are restless until they find their rest in thee." In this famous prayer the creation-faith is understood in its vertical dimension: man's being is constituted by relationship with God. Outside that relationship which defines his nature, his "person-ness," he leads an inauthentic and finally meaningless existence.

In our time the existentialist interpretation of creation has found wide support. It is advocated, for instance, by Alan Richardson in his commentary on Genesis 1–11.[7] Richardson objects to calling the creation stories "myths" because, in popular parlance, this suggests that there was no real act of creation at all. "God *did* create the world," he writes. "This is no myth. Similarly man's condition *is* fallen: there is, alas, no question of myth here."[8] On the other hand, the language used in Genesis 1–11 is completely different from that of a scientific textbook.

> The truth with which [the creation stories] deal is not of the same order as the truth with which history and geography, astronomy and geology, deal; it is not the literal truth of the actual observation of measurable things and events; it is ultimate truth, the truth which can be grasped only by the imagination, and which can be expressed only by image and symbolism.[9]

Therefore, he proposes to consider these stories as "parables," to be read as poetry, not prose. Although one might object that, form-critically, this is a very loose usage of the genre "parable," one must see that the central point Richardson

---

[7] Alan Richardson, *Genesis I–XI* [130]. See also the essays on creation by Rudolf Bultmann [167].

[8] *Ibid.,* p. 28.

[9] *Ibid.,* p. 30.

makes regarding religious language is important. Even those, like Karl Barth, who advocate a *heilsgeschichtliche* view of creation as the first of God's historical acts, would have to acknowledge that this first event, which lies at the remote boundary of history, can be portrayed only in symbols of religious imagination. In this case, however, Richardson seems to put the accent in a different place than *Heilsgeschichte*. The parables of Genesis, he says, contain a special kind of truth: "the truth of religious awareness." It is the kind of truth which cannot be expressed in philosophical, theological, or psychological terms, for that, he says, "would be to transpose it into one of the other orders of truth, to depersonalize it."

The intention of the parables of the *Urgeschichte*, according to this understanding, is to express the existential awareness that my origin, my being, my destiny are subject to the will of God, not governed by my own will. As some existentialist theologians would put it, the self is "a derived self." Says Richardson:

> The parables of Creation do not offer us a theory, a philosophical hypothesis, of how the world came into existence; nor does the parable of the Fall offer us a scientific analysis of human nature. On the contrary, they offer me personal knowledge about my existence, my dependence upon God, my alienation from him, my need of reconciliation to him.[10]

He goes on to say that implicit in this existential knowledge of "myself-in-relation-to-God" are certain "general truths"—truths about the universe, about the earth, about human nature. But these general truths are inferences from the truth of *my* existence.

> Only if I have *first* perceived that this existential truth applies to *me*, shall I comprehend that such general truths for philosophy and theology are involved in the Genesis stories. I must first understand that I am Adam, made in God's likeness, rebelling against his purpose, desiring to be "as God." The Genesis parables certainly carry many and deep implications concerning mankind in

---

10 *Ibid.*, p. 30.

general, but I shall not understand this until I have first come to
know that they are addressed to the particular Adam which is
myself.[11]

So interpreted, the creation stories are not just about the
past but about the present. *Urgeschichte* refers not merely to
primeval history but *primal* history, that is, to the historicity
which is constitutive of the human person. The element *Ur*
("original," "primal") is a description of man's historical being—the being of the person who knows existentially that his
life originates with God, even as he also knows that sin is
original with him! While one may question whether this interpretation does full justice to the view of history expressed
in the creation-faith, it surely cannot be denied that contemporaneity is an important dimension of the biblical stories.
These stories purport to be our story. It is well known that the
Hebrew word *'Adam* is a generic term for "man, mankind."
As the old Jewish proverb says, Everyman is Adam.[12] Accordingly, the German theologian Helmut Thielicke, whose dynamic preaching in a Hamburg cathedral has reverberated far
beyond his own city and country, is justified in regarding the
language of Genesis 1–11 (the primeval history) as fundamentally "parabolic symbolism" and in interpreting these stories
as a searching exposé of human life itself. Commenting on the
first two verses of Genesis, which portray an earth without
form and void and the beginning of God's creative work, he
remarks that the interest of this story could hardly have been
scientific; "otherwise we would surely see in it the attempt to
drive the drill still deeper into the bedrock of the world and
go back behind the world of creation." Rather, "the first pages
of the Bible," he insists, "have a totally different interest."

Their purpose is to show what it means for me and my life that
God is there at the beginning and at the end, and that everything

---

11 *Ibid.*, pp. 30–31.

12 "Adam is therefore not the cause, save only of his own soul, but each
of us has been the Adam of his own soul." Syriac Apocalypse of Baruch
54:19; found in R. H. Charles, *Apocrypha and Pseudepigrapha of the Old
Testament* [4].

that happens in the world—my little life with its cares and its joys, and also the history of the world at large extending from stone-age man to the atomic era—that all of this is, so to speak, a discourse enclosed, upheld, and guarded by the breath of God.[13]

This is in line with Luther's Shorter Catechism, where he states that the creedal affirmation that God is Maker of heaven and earth boils down essentially to this: I believe that God is *my* creator.

It is not difficult to move from the creation story, so interpreted, to biblical psalms which express man's wonder about his being alive and the greater wonder that God is mindful of him. Psalm 8, which is related in some way to the Priestly creation account of Genesis 1, is an eloquent witness to the meaning of the creation-faith in the liturgy of Israel's worship. This hymn begins and ends with an exclamation of praise to God's glory and majesty which, to the eye of faith, are evident in the beauty of the world and in the astonishing order of the universe. The psalmist knows that while adults come to take this world for granted, the little child responds with spontaneous and elemental joy to the works of God. And yet he knows too, that praise is the sign that man is alive, that he is fully human. For man lives vis-à-vis God, his creator.

> When I look at thy heavens, the work of thy fingers,
>   the moon and the stars which thou has established;
>   what is man that thou art mindful of him,
>   and the son of man that thou dost care for him?
>   —PSALM 8:3–4

Here the creation-faith focuses upon the relationship between God and man. It is not just that man, in contrast to the God who has spread out the star-studded canopy of the heavens, is transient and finite. As the book of Ecclesiastes shows, the awareness of the gulf fixed between Creator and creature can prompt a melancholy feeling of insignificance and emptiness. Rather, the creation-faith brings to man an understanding of his existence—the awareness that "his relationship with God

---

13 Helmut Thielicke, *How the World Began* [148], pp. 13 f.

is that of an *incomprehensible grace*." [14] The wonder of wonders, which evokes the psalmist's praise, is that the Almighty
God who spread out the heavens and created the innumerable
starry host is actually mindful of his small creature and, even
more astounding, that he confers upon him the honor of ex-
ercising dominion over the earth as his representative, as one
who is made but a "little less than God." Praise rises to a climax as the psalmist draws upon the old cultic tradition found
also in the Priestly creation story:

> Yet thou has made him little less than God,
>   and dost crown him with glory and honor.
> Thou hast given him dominion over the works of thy hands;
>   thou hast put all things under his feet . . .[15]
>
> —PSALM 8:5–6

In this psalm, man's God-given commission to govern the
world means specifically to subdue the animals and to use
them for his benefit. But surely it is appropriate to understand
this dominion in a larger sense: the conquest of nature by
man's science and the exploration of the realms of space which
lie beyond the earth. The modern age has accentuated man's
sense of smallness. Man is a faceless individual in a vast and
lonely industrial crowd, a mere infinitesimal speck on the surface of the dust globule called the earth. Today we can ask
the psalmist's question with great passion: Can it be that the
God whose glory fills the universe is *really* interested in his
creature? And if this question is answered affirmatively, as it is
in this psalm and in the whole Bible, then praise should manifest itself in our work, whatever it is, whether turning a nut
in an assembly line, plowing the soil with a tractor, mending
clothes, or manning a spaceship.

This sense that man is not only creaturely but dependent
upon God's grace is, by extension, the basis of "general truths"

---

14 Artur Weiser, commentary on Ps. 8, in *The Psalms* [154].
15 Cf. Gen. 1:26–28. There the "image of God" also conveys the idea of
a special relationship with God which entitles man to exercise dominion
as God's representative. On this point, see Gerhard von Rad's commentary
on this passage [124].

concerning the world, the animals, and the creatures in the universe. Therefore in the Psalter the invitation to praise God reaches out beyond man, in whom praise becomes articulate, to all of God's creatures. So in Psalm 148 the sun, moon and stars; the sea monsters and the deeps; lightning and hail, snow and frost; mountains and hills, beasts and cattle—everything and everyone join in the great anthem of praise to the glory of God.

> All thy works shall praise thee, O Yahweh,
> and all thy saints shall bless thee!
> —PSALM 145:10

Thus man's understanding of his own existence as God's creature is mirrored in and confirmed by what he sees all around him in the world. All creatures exist within the relationship of God's incomprehensible grace.

III

In view of what has been said about the "vertical" or existential dimension of creation we should not be surprised to find that the psalms which are usually designated as "creation-psalms"—namely, Psalm 8 (which we have already considered) and Psalms 19A and 104—display no interest in *Heilsgeschichte:* Israel's sacred history. The first part of Psalm 19 (part A = vss. 1–6) is a good illustration. Although the psalm in its present form is firmly anchored in Israel's faith, owing to the praise of the Torah with which it concludes (part B = vss. 7–14), the first part is neutral in regard to the historical faith of Israel.[16] It even employs the old Semitic word for deity, El—not the special name of Israel's God, Yahweh.

> The heavens are telling the glory of God ['El];
> and the firmament proclaims his handiwork.

---

[16] In its present form, however, Ps. 19 reflects a late stage in Israelite faith when God's revelation was identified with his giving of the Torah, in contrast to the earlier emphasis upon Yahweh's historical acts; and at this stage Torah theology and Wisdom-theology tended to blend together. See J. C. Rylaarsdam, *Revelation in Jewish Wisdom Literature* [139]. Another psalm of this type is Ps. 1.

Day to day pours forth speech,
   and night to night declares knowledge.
There is no speech, nor are there words;
   their voice is not heard;
yet their voice [?] goes out through all the earth,[17]
   and their words to the end of the world.
                                        —Psalm 19:1–4a

It is important to notice that here the psalmist does not say
that God is revealed in nature; rather the heavens are *witnesses* to his glory. The Nineteenth Psalm, as Henri Frankfort
reminded us (see above, p. 32), intends to emphasize the transcendence of God, and therefore it "mocks the beliefs of Babylonians and Egyptians" who conceived the divine as "immanent in nature." In the psalmist's faith the creation points
beyond itself to the Creator, upon whom all things and all
beings are dependent. The light which suffuses the creation is
God's *kabod* ("glory"), the refulgent radiance which shields
his being. The marvelous order of the universe bears witness to
God's artistry, to the work of his hands. And throughout the
creation rings nature's silent anthem of praise, which is repeated from day to day and night to night without cessation.
With poetic freedom the psalmist draws upon pagan mythological motifs, such as the view that the sun-god has his abode in
the sea, where at night he rests in the embrace of his lover,
only to emerge from the bridal chamber in the morning with
youthful vigor and radiant splendor. This mythological imagery, however, is converted to the metaphorical language of
praise.

In them [perhaps, "in the sea"] he has set a tent for the sun,
which comes forth like a bridegroom leaving his chamber,
   and like a strong man runs its course with joy.
Its rising is from the end of the heavens,
   and its circuit to the end of them;
   and there is nothing hid from its heat.
                                        —Psalm 19:4b–6

---

[17] The translation "their voice," which is based on Jerome's Vulgate, is
uncertain. See the commentaries.

To the psalmist the sun is only one of God's creatures which obediently performs its appointed task and thereby joins the heavenly anthem of praise to the sublime majesty of the Creator.

The same accent is found in Psalm 104, a prayer addressed to Yahweh the God of Israel which—as we have already observed (on pp. 48–49)—is strikingly similar in spirit and wording to Akhnaton's hymn to the Aton as the sole creator and renewer of life. The psalmist is filled with a profound sense of wonder as he surveys the whole range of God's creation. The scope of thought is matched by the creation story of Genesis 1. Indeed, the sequence is so similar that probably we should assume that both passages reflect the liturgical practice of the Jerusalem temple.[18] Notice how the seven strophes parallel the Genesis account:

i

| 104:1–4 | In traditional language the psalmist speaks first of the creation of the heavens. God's heavenly palace has been firmly established upon the cosmic ocean above the firmament. Light, clouds, wind, and fire display his cosmic majesty. | Cf. Gen. 1:6–8 |

ii

| 104:5–9 | God has firmly established the earth by pushing back the waters of chaos and establishing bounds for them, so that chaos would not engulf the earth. The old myth of the creator's victory over the rebellious powers of chaos is used more freely in Psalm 104 than in the Genesis account. | Cf. Gen. 1:9–10 |

18 See further P. Humbert's article dealing with the relation of Gen. 1 and Ps. 104 to the New Year festival [78]. In view of its affinities with the Egyptian "Hymn to the Sun," Psalm 104 may be relatively early and prior to Gen. 1 in literary formulation, in which case perhaps the Priestly account is dependent on it. So Samuel Terrien ([146], p. 123), who stresses that the hymn expresses "a theology of creative omnipotence which has radically transformed the implications of mythical language" (p. 121).

Note the conflict language: "At thy rebuke they [the waters of chaos] fled . . ."
(vs. 7).

iii

104:10–13	The waters of chaos, having been tamed, were converted to beneficial use. The water gushes up from underground springs and rains down from heaven.	(Implied in Gen. 1:6–10)

iv

104:14–18	The result is that vegetation grows, which in turn makes life possible for birds, beasts, and man.	Cf. Gen. 1:11–12

v

104:19–23	God created the moon and the sun to reckon the times, so that the beasts may find their food in the night and man may perform his work during the day.	Cf. Gen. 1:14–18

vi

104:24–26	The psalmist reflects upon the remnant of watery chaos, the sea, with its teeming creatures great and small. Leviathan is no longer the dreaded monster of chaos but God's "plaything" (cf. Job 41:5).	Cf. Gen. 1:20–22

vii

104:27–30	The dependence of man and animals upon God for life.	Cf. Gen. 1:24–30

While the Genesis story culminates with God's creating man
in his image (cf. Ps. 8:5: "lacking but a little") and investing
him with dominion over the earth, Psalm 104 moves toward
an exclamation of wonder about the dependence of life—ani-
mal and human—upon the Creator.

These all look to thee,
to give them their food in due season.
When thou givest to them, they gather it up;
when thou openest thy hand, they are filled with good things.

When thou hidest thy face, they are dismayed;
  when thou takest away their breath, they die
  and return to their dust.
When thou sendest forth thy Spirit [lit., "breath"], they are
    created; [19]
  and thou renewest the face of the ground.

                    —PSALM 104:27–30

The Hebrew verbs (imperfects) describe actions that continue, thus indicating that God's creation is a continual sustaining and renewing activity. The intention of Psalm 104, Gerhard von Rad observes, is "to show how the whole world is open to God—in every moment of its existence it requires to be sustained by God, everything 'waits' on him (vs. 27); and it also receives this sustenance all the time. Were Yahweh to turn away from the world even for just one moment, then its splendour would immediately collapse (vs. 29)." [20]

In his oratorio *The Creation,* Haydn appropriately placed a paraphrase of these verses at the point of the sixth day of creation (Gen. 1:31), when God saw everything that he had made and called it very good.

IV

These creation-psalms, as we have observed, show no interest in *Heilsgeschichte.* They may have entered Israelite tradition via the wisdom schools which, at least from the time of Solomon, increasingly influenced Israelite life and worship. It is noteworthy, however, that in other psalms that have the theme of deliverance from death, the old creation imagery is used to portray the *redemptive* activity of God. In these cases, too, it may be said that creation is understood existentially, but the thought shifts from an awareness of the creature's dependence

---

[19] The verb translated "they are created" is a form of the same verb used in Gen. 1:1 *(bara').* This verb is used only of God's creative activity and its accusative is always the product of God's action, never the material out of which something is formed.

[20] *Old Testament Theology* [126], Vol. I, p. 361.

upon the Creator to an existential cry "out of the depths" to
the God who alone can save. In other words, the interest is
soteriological.

Here we may recall the various psalms in which a suppliant
portrays his distress in the imagery of being engulfed by "deep
waters" or as a descent into the waters of the Deep.[21] This is
the case in the psalm inserted into the book of Jonah and occasioned by his sojourn in the belly of a fish (Jonah 2:2–9).

> "I called to Yahweh, out of my distress,
>   and he answered me;
> out of the belly of Sheol I cried,
>   and thou didst hear my voice.
> For thou didst cast me into the deep,
>   into the heart of the seas,
>   and the flood was round about me;
> all thy waves and thy billows
>   passed over me."
>
> —JONAH 2:2–3

Here Sheol is pictured as a pit beneath the earth, surrounded
by the waters of the subterranean ocean. This picture, however, should not be converted into a literal spatial location.
Since, in the ancient way of thinking, water signified the dimension of the chaotic (we would say, perhaps, "nonbeing"),
it was appropriate to conceive death, the great threat to life,
as having its abode within the Deep.

These descriptions presuppose a view of life and death which
is strange to the modern world. We tend to diagnose the difference between life and death in physical terms. Death, we
think, occurs in that instant when bodily functions cease and
consciousness goes out like a light. The Israelite, however,
viewed death as a weak form of life, as a decrease in "the vitality of the individual."[22] Any threat to a person's *shalom*
("welfare"), whether from sickness, weakness, imprisonment,

---

21 For this type of water imagery, see such passages as Pss. 18:4–5; 32:6;
42:7; 69:1–2, 14–15; 88:6–7; 124:3–5; 144:7; Job 38:16–17; cf. Isa. 43:2.

22 A. R. Johnson, *The Vitality of the Individual in the Thought of Ancient Israel* [84].

or attack by enemies, was felt to be an encroachment of death
into the land of the living. The Israelite view of the universe,
as the Scandinavian scholar Johannes Pedersen reminds us, is
a dramatic conception of "the fight for life against death."

> The land of life lies in the centre, on all hands surrounded by the
> land of death. The wilderness lies outside, the realm of death and
> the ocean below, but they send in their tentacles from all sides,
> and make the world a mixture of life and death, of light and dark-
> ness. But life *must* be the stronger. The great terror of the Israelite
> is that some day evil shall get the upper hand, and chaos come to
> prevail in the world of man.[23]

Thus the Israelite knew existentially that the domain of death
could extend into "the land of the living," the realm of history. And above all, in the Israelite view death means separation from God. "Death begins to become a reality," observes
von Rad, "at the point where Yahweh forsakes a man, where
he is silent, i.e. at whatever point the life-relationship with
Yahweh wears thin." [24]
Therefore the psalmists often describe their experience of
the absence of God, of God-forsakeness, as a descent into Sheol
where there is no life precisely because in that dark region the
"shades" [25] do not praise God. Psalm 88 is a typical lament.
The psalmist portrays himself as "a man who has no strength,"
who is reckoned among those who go down to the Pit (Sheol).

> Thou hast put me in the depths of the Pit,
>   in the regions dark and deep.
> Thy wrath lies heavy upon me,
>   and thou dost overwhelm me with all thy waves.
>   —Psalm 88:6–7

---

23 Johannes Pedersen, *Israel: Its Life and Culture* [122], I–II, pp. 470 f.
24 *Theology of the Old Testament* [126], Vol. I, p. 388.
25 A person's shade is his ghost, that is, the person reduced to the weak-
est form of vitality. The Old Testament rejects the view prevalent in the
ancient Near East that the shades had sufficient vitality to do good or evil,
a belief which was the basis of necromancy. Notice, however, the tradition
that Saul, though having banished mediums, clandestinely consulted the
witch of Endor, who summoned from Sheol Samuel's shade (I Sam. 28).

To him the bitterness of dying is that death means separation from God, for in Sheol there is no proclamation of Yahweh's saving work in history.

> Dost thou work wonders for the dead?
>   Do the shades rise up to praise thee?
> Is thy steadfast love declared in the grave,
>   or thy faithfulness in Abaddon?
> Are thy wonders known in the darkness,
>   or thy saving help in the land of forgetfulness?
>   —PSALM 88:10–12

Since death, or its imminence, is a threat to the meaning of man's life in history, it was appropriate for psalmists to turn to creation-versus-chaos imagery—the imagery of Genesis 1 which contrasts the darkness and confusion of chaos with the ordered world of light and life.[26] It is interesting, however, to see how psalmists also employed this same creation imagery, even with its mythological features, to describe "the epiphany of God" to deliver—a prominent motif in many psalms.[27] A psalmist tells how, when the snares of death were encompassing him, Yahweh came to the rescue in an earth-shaking epiphany (Ps. 18 = II Sam. 22). So violent was the storm which accompanied his coming that the creation was shaken to its very foundations. The vivid description (Ps. 18: 7–15) includes these lines:

> Yahweh also thundered in the heavens,
>   and the Most High ['Elyon] uttered his voice,
>   hailstones and coals of fire.
> And he sent out his arrows, and scattered them;
>   he flashed forth lightnings, and routed them.
> Then the channels of Sea [Yam] [28] were seen,

---

26 See Aubrey Johnson, "Jonah 2.3–10: A Study in Cultic Phantasy" [83], p. 89.

27 See C. Westermann, *The Praise of God in the Psalms* [157], pp. 93–98.

28 Ps. 18 at this point has "waters" but the parallel text in II Sam. 22:16 has "sea" (without the article), which is unquestionably correct. See Frank M. Cross and David N. Freedman, "A Royal Song of Thanksgiving" [31], p. 26.

and the foundations of the world were laid bare,
  at thy rebuke, O Yahweh,
    at the blast of the breath of thy nostrils.
         —PSALM 18:13–15

Here the poet draws heavily upon traditional storm-god symbolism, such as the portrayal of Baal's battle against Sea *(Yam)* and River *(Nahar)* or Marduk's mounting his storm chariot and using the winds and the lightning as his weapons.[29] According to the psalmist, the purpose of the coming of Elyon, the creator (see above, pp. 69–71), was to redeem from the "strong enemy."

He reached from on high, he took me,
  he drew me out of many waters.
He delivered me from my strong enemy,
  and from those who hated me;
    for they were too mighty for me.
         —PSALM 18:16–17

The expression *many waters* (or *mighty waters*), here and often in the psalms of Israel, refers to the insurgent waters of chaos, as Herbert May has shown; and the imagery is used here to show the divine triumph over enemies that threaten the king and the people (see vs. 50).[30] Thus the subterranean waters through which one must pass in the descent to Sheol are identified with the hostile waters of chaos. And the victory over menacing death comes from Yahweh, who triumphs over the waters.

The motif of "the epiphany of God" is developed in a striking manner in the psalm of Habakkuk (Chap. 3)—a passage which echoes mythological elements found in Ras Shamra texts. The psalm, after an initial address (3:2), presents a vivid description of Yahweh's epiphany for the purpose of obtaining

---

29 See Herbert G. May, "Some Cosmic Connotations of *Mayim Rabbim,* 'Many Waters' " [100], p. 14. He also draws attention to the parallel of the Hittite myth in which the storm god defeats the dragon Illuyankas; see *Ancient Near Eastern Texts* [5], pp. 125–26.

30 "The 'many waters' are the chaotic, disorderly, insurgent elements which must be controlled" (H. G. May [100], p. 10).

victory for his people and his "anointed," that is, the king (vss. 3–15). From afar he came to the rescue, accompanied by such a violent storm that the everlasting mountains supporting the earth were leveled. His coming on his storm chariot to vanquish the enemies threatening his people is portrayed as a dramatic conflict with the waters of chaos.

> Was thy wrath against the rivers [neharim], O Yahweh?
> > Was thy anger against the rivers,
> > > or thy indignation against the sea [Yam],
> > when thou didst ride upon thy horses,
> > > upon thy chariot of victory?
>
> —HABAKKUK 3:8

The poet says that when Yahweh charged forth in his chariot, with his lightning arrows poised to shoot and his glittering spear flashing, the mountains supporting the earth writhed and *Tehom* ("Deep") cried out in panic (vs. 10). Here there is such obvious dependence upon the Canaanite myth of Baal's fierce battle with Prince Sea and Ruler River that originally the Hebrew text must have read "Sea" rather than "the sea" (with the definite article):

> Thou didst trample Sea with thy horses,
> > the surging of mighty [or "many"] waters.
> > > —HABAKKUK 3:15

However, the chaos imagery is appropriated in this psalm to show Yahweh's historical victory for his people (cf. Ps. 89:9–10) as in the days of old—the time of the Exodus—when he marched from the region of Sinai toward Edom (Hab. 3:7).[31]

> Thou didst bestride the earth in fury,
> > thou didst trample the nations in anger.
> Thou wentest forth for the salvation of thy people,
> > for the salvation of thy anointed.
> > > —HABAKKUK 3:12–13a

---

[31] Herbert May, in his illuminating discussion of Hab. 3 and related passages [100], draws attention to the fact that Yahweh's domination of the dragon of chaos (Rahab, "the sea," "the rivers" ["floods"], "many waters") is synonymous with his triumph over Israel's or Yahweh's enemies at the Reed Sea or in subsequent historical crises.

Therefore the psalmist, recollecting Yahweh's saving acts of old, can wait in quiet confidence for his deliverance from foes and can trust him absolutely.

> Though the fig tree do not blossom,
>   nor fruit be on the vines,
> the produce of the olive fail
>   and the fields yield no food,
> the flock be cut off from the fold
>   and there be no herd in the stalls,
> yet I will rejoice in Yahweh,
>   I will joy in the God of my salvation.
>   —HABAKKUK 3:17–18

V

It is clear from these psalms that the creation-faith is not just the awareness of the creature's radical dependence upon the Creator; it is also an expression of confidence in the Creator's power to save, of his rulership over the tumultuous forces of history. Creation-faith in this dynamic sense is expressed in a number of psalms whose central motif is the kingship of Yahweh over the nations and the whole cosmos. Not only is Yahweh praised as "maker of the heavens" (Ps. 96:5) but he is acclaimed as enthroned triumphantly over the restless and rebellious waters of chaos. According to Psalm 93, which is typical of these so-called "Enthronement Psalms," [32] Yahweh's throne was established primordially—"from of old."

> Yahweh reigns [or "Yahweh is King!"]; he is robed in majesty;
>   Yahweh is robed, he is girded with strength.
> Yea, the world is established; it shall never be moved;
>   thy throne is established from of old;
>   thou art from everlasting.
>   —PSALM 93:1–2

Then the psalmist praises Yahweh for his victory over the chaotic powers of the cosmos:

---

[32] Scholars differ in the number of psalms to be placed in this category, but at least the following should be included: Pss. 47, 93, 96, 97, 98, 99.

> The floods [*neharoth*] [33] have lifted up, O Yahweh,
>   the floods have lifted up their voice,
>   the floods lift up their roaring.
> Mightier than the thunders of many waters,
>   mightier than the waves of the sea,
>   Yahweh on high is mighty!
>
> —PSALM 93:3–4

According to another Enthronement Psalm, the waters of chaos have become so tamed and transformed that, instead of being hostile to Yahweh, they roar their acclaim of the king.

> Let the sea roar, and all that fills it;
>   the world and those who dwell in it!
> Let the floods [*neharoth*] clap their hands;
>   let the hills sing for joy together
> before Yahweh, for he comes
>   to rule the earth.
> He will judge the world with righteousness,
>   and the peoples with equity.
>
> —PSALM 98:7–9

The Enthronement Psalms are the product of the Jerusalem cult, which, as we have noticed previously (on pp. 60–68), was a crucible in which Israel's ancient historical faith was blended with elements of Canaanite, Babylonian, and Egyptian mythology. The Canaanite element in the Enthronement Psalms is attested by another psalm which begins by summoning the members of the Heavenly Council ("the sons of Gods") to praise Yahweh, God of storm. The storm described in this psalm is not just the phenomenon known in Palestine, for the "thunder" (voice) of Yahweh is upon "many waters." [34]

---

[33] This is the feminine plural of "river," a word which appears in the masculine plural *(neharim)* in Hab. 3:8. The singular *(nahar)* is the same as one of the names of the adversary of Baal in the Ugaritic mythology, namely, "Ruler *River*."

[34] In this connection, May ([100], p. 16) calls attention to Nah. 1:3–4, where Yahweh, coming in whirlwind and storm, "rebukes the sea" and dries up "all the rivers *(neharoth)*."

The voice of Yahweh is upon the waters;
the God of glory thunders,
Yahweh, upon many waters.
The voice of Yahweh is powerful,
the voice of Yahweh is full of majesty.
—PSALM 29:3–4

The psalm reaches a climax by proclaiming that Yahweh, having won his victory over the chaotic waters, sits enthroned over the flood.

Yahweh sits enthroned over the flood [*mabbul*];
Yahweh sits enthroned as king for ever.
—PSALM 29:10

Clearly we have here an old Canaanite hymn which was taken over by Israel and converted to the Yahweh faith.[35] Since this appropriation must have taken place early in the period of the monarchy, it is unnecessary to say, as have some scholars (e.g. Kraus, Westermann), that the Enthronement Psalms come from the post-exilic period when they were influenced by Second Isaiah.

Many scholars, following the lead of Sigmund Mowinckel, have assigned these psalms to a cultic *Sitz im Leben*, namely, the Feast of Tabernacles or the New Year feast in Jerusalem, when Yahweh's kingship was celebrated by rehearsing his victory over the waters of chaos. It has even been proposed that the cultic shout *Yahweh malak*, found, for instance, in 93:1 and 96:10 (RSV "The Lord reigns"), should be translated "Yahweh has become king," [36] in which case there would be a parallel to the Babylonian New Year festival, when Marduk's elevation to supreme rulership in the assembly of the gods prompted the shout "Marduk has become king!" or perhaps to a similar ceremony in Canaan (Ugarit) when the cry "Let Baal reign!" was

---

35 On the Canaanite character of the psalm, see for instance articles by Louis Ginzberg [64] and Frank M. Cross [33].

36 So Sigmund Mowinckel especially. See his work *The Psalms in Israel's Worship* [109], especially pp. 106–92, "Psalms at the Enthronement Festival of Yahweh"; see also his earlier *Psalmenstudien* [108], which opened a new phase in the study of the Psalms.

raised. While it is possible to translate the Hebrew verb (a perfect) in this sense ("Yahweh has become king") this translation is exegetically dubious; for in contrast to Marduk's or Baal's dominion, Yahweh's kingship is not subject to the seasonal cycle of summer barrenness and fertility, of death and resurrection. Undoubtedly the exclamation should be rendered "Yahweh is king!" Nevertheless, these psalms show that Israel appropriated mythological elements from the pagan environment and reinterpreted them to express Yahweh's cosmic kingship and universal sway over the nations. It is quite probable that during the period of the monarchy there was an annual festival in Jerusalem, held in the fall at the turn of the year, when pilgrims celebrated Yahweh's kingship as well as the founding of Zion and the election of the Davidic king. An echo of this great pilgrimage festival is heard in a late (post-exilic) passage in the book of Zechariah which states that those who survive the final battle of history "shall go up year after year to worship the King, Yahweh of hosts, and to keep the feast of booths [tabernacles]," and that the penalty for failure to observe this custom would be no rainfall (Zech. 14:16–17).[37]

It is likely—to recall what was said in the previous chapter—that the Jerusalem festival to which these psalms belonged was infused with royal covenant theology. There the anointed Davidic king was regarded as the agent and representative of the King par excellence who was enthroned "high and lifted up"—as Isaiah perceived in a vision in the temple, possibly in connection with an enthronement festival (Isa. 6:1–5). According to this belief, the order which Yahweh created at the beginning, when he established the world on its foundation so that it would never be moved (cf. Ps. 96:10), is mediated through the king to society. The king, like God, who has elected him, performs the role of a judge (shofeṭ), that is, he upholds order by administering justice and by defeating Israel's enemies, the

---

[37] The holding of this festival on the eve of the coming of the winter rains suggests to John Gray (The Legacy of Canaan [66], pp. 21, 33–34) that at Ugarit too an enthronement festival was celebrated, when Baal was worshiped as lord of storm and rain.

two major functions of rulership.[38] Thus in the so-called "Royal Psalms," such as Psalms 2 and 110, the king is assured of victory over enemies, and this victory was apparently understood as a repetition of the divine victory in the beginning. In Israel's cult the "cosmic drama" of creation, as Paul Ricoeur discerningly observes, has become a "messianic drama" of history, in which the Anointed (the "messiah," i.e. the reigning king) battles the enemy who is none other than the primordial enemy in historical guise.[39] Yahweh says to his Anointed: "I will set his hand on the sea and his right hand on the rivers" (Ps. 89:25). And in a time of distress the Davidic king prays to Yahweh to come in an epiphany of storm and deliver him "from the many waters, from the hand of aliens" (Ps. 144:5–8).

VI

In pagan festivals, of course, the events that occurred "in the beginning" were cultically contemporized. The victory over the waters of chaos was not a liturgical metaphor; this was, in the faith of archaic man, an event in which he participated. The divine victory was reenacted, with the king playing a central role in the ritual combat. In view of the striking parallels between Israel's psalms and ancient mythological texts it may well be that the Israelite celebration of Yahweh's kingship had a similar sacramental significance. This is the view of the Scandinavian scholar Helmer Ringgren, who takes up the suggestion of Johannes Pedersen that for an Israelite "to remember a thing" meant that it "becomes an active reality in the life of the believer." [40] Ringgren draws attention to various passages

---

38 The Hebrew verb *shafaṭ* (e.g. Ps. 98:9) often has a broader meaning than our word *judge*—as in the book of Judges. This is true also in the Ras Shamra texts, where the adversary is known as Ruler ("judge") River or where Baal is acclaimed as Ruler: "Our King is Baal the Mighty, Our Ruler ("judge") above whom there is none." Cited in J. Gray, *The Legacy of Canaan* [66], p. 49.

39 See Paul Ricoeur, *The Symbolism of Evil* [132], the entire discussion of the role of the Hebrew king in Pt. II, Chap. I.

40 Helmer Ringgren, *The Faith of the Psalmists* [133], especially p. 19.

in the Psalter which refer to *seeing* God's mighty deeds. For instance,

> Come and see what God has done:
> he is terrible in his deeds among men.
>   —PSALM 66:5

or:

> Come, behold the works of the Lord,
> how he has wrought desolations in the earth.
>   —PSALM 46:8

Whatever we make of the notion of a "cultic drama," he says, there must have been a cultic actualization of God's *ḥesed* through the remembrance of the past. We do not have to subscribe to the theory of an enthronement festival celebrated at the turn of the New Year to recognize that the book of Psalms reflects cultic experiences of the worshiping people. "It is very probable," he writes, "that there were cultic ceremonies, in which the Lord was celebrated as the Creator, the King, and the Judge of the world, and that the mythological or historical events connected with these concepts were symbolically represented or enacted in some way." In other words, the creation imagery of the victory over the waters of chaos was something more than metaphorical language to express Yahweh's absolute Lordship and the dependence of the whole creation upon his sovereign will. This language, at least in some of the psalms, points to *events* which were cultically remembered.

In recent years a great deal of attention has been given to *Vergegenwärtigung* (often translated "re-presentation" or "actualization"), that is, making the past present.[41] These discussions are based on the recognition that it is not enough to say that biblical faith finds expression in the telling of a story, the

---

See also E. Jacob, *Theology of the Old Testament* [81], p. 267, who thinks it likely that the cult included "dramatic representations of the great events of the past," the purpose being "the overcoming of chronological and spacial distance and the real introduction of the onlookers into the presence of the God who not only acted there and then, but who still acts *hic et nunc*."

[41] See, for instance, the essay on "The 'Re-presentation' of the Old Testament in Proclamation," by Martin Noth [118].

recitation of a *Heilsgeschichte*. If an event has significance for faith, if it is a crucial event for the believing community, it should be possible to contemporize it, especially in the context of worship. An excellent illustration is the cultic celebration of the Eucharist or Holy Communion, when worshipers relive and reenact the sacrifice of Christ. And in Jewish worship the redemptive event of the Exodus is one in which every generation is involved. The Passover Haggadah says:

> In every generation one must look upon himself as if he personally had come forth from Egypt, in keeping with the Biblical command, "And thou shalt tell thy son in that day, saying, it is because of that which the Lord did to *me* when I went forth from Egypt." For it was not alone our fathers whom the Holy One, blessed be He, redeemed, but also us whom He redeemed with them, as it is said, "And *us* He brought out thence that He might lead *us* to, and give *us*, the land which He swore to our fathers." [42]

The question is, What would be meant, within the context of Israelite faith, by the announcement that Yahweh's victory over the powers of chaos was an event—a crucial event—in which the worshiping community participated? Probably this question should be answered by saying that within the Israelite cult a great shift took place from a mythical event to a historical event "in the beginning." Paul Ricoeur understands this "demythologizing" well:

> A purely historical combat takes the place of the theogonic combat. The Exodus—that is to say, the departure from Egypt—the key event of the whole Biblical theology of history, has acquired a consistency of its own, a new signification with regard to the primordial creation; it is an event without any reference in principle to any drama of creation. . . . It is history, and no longer the drama of creation, that becomes the active center of symbolism.

And the consequence of this shift from the drama of creation to the drama of history, he continues, is that the enemy is no

---

42 *The Haggadah of the Passover*, ed. by David and Tamar de Sola Pool (Bloch, 1953), p. 51. See also Will Herberg, "Beyond Time and Eternity: Reflections on Passover and Easter" [74].

longer primeval chaos in the mythical sense but, rather, "undergoes a sort of reduction to the purely historical." [43]

We can see the evidences of this drastic shift of emphasis in the literature of Israel. The creation-faith of Israel, though heavily dependent upon mythological and cultic traditions of the ancient world, witnesses to a decisive, non-repeatable *historical event* of the past, which marked a new beginning. It is not surprising, then, that in various psalms Yahweh's victory over the waters of chaos is historicized, as in the prayer of Habakkuk which we have already discussed (on pp. 97–99). This creative event was identified with the *crucial event* of Yahweh's victory at the Reed Sea, the event which marked the beginning of Israel's history. In an early tradition about the crossing of the sea, the "Song of the Sea" in Exodus 15, Yahweh's enemies are the hosts of Pharaoh. The sea is merely the passive instrument by which Yahweh won his victory on behalf of Israel. But in other poems of a later origin the waters of the Reed Sea are none other than the waters of chaos. Yahweh's battle was fought not in the timeless realm of mythology but in the arena of history—namely, at the beginning, when Israel was created to be his people. Thus Psalm 77, a lament which recalls Yahweh's mighty deeds of old when he redeemed his people, says that:

> When the waters saw thee, O God,
>   when the waters saw thee, they were afraid,
>   yea, the deeps [tehomoth] trembled.
> The clouds poured out waters;
>   the skies gave forth thunder;
>   thy arrows flashed on every side.
> The crash of thy thunder was in the whirlwind;
>   thy lightnings lighted up the world;
>   the earth trembled and shook.
>   —PSALM 77:16–18

But the concluding verses of this lament indicate when the victory was won: it was at the crossing of the Reed Sea.[44]

---

43 P. Ricoeur [132], Pt. II, Chap. I.

44 May ([100], pp. 12–13) discusses the literary parallels between Ps. 77 and Hab. 3.

Thy way was through the sea,
  thy path through the great [or "many"] waters;
  yet thy footprints were unseen.
Thou didst lead thy people like a flock
  by the hand of Moses and Aaron.
                    —PSALM 77:19–20

Mythical imagery also appears in Psalm 74, a lament which
was composed in the shadow of a great national disaster, presumably the destruction of Jerusalem in 587 B.C. The psalmist
appeals to God to remember the congregation which he has
"created" (RSV: "gotten") of old and Mount Zion which has
been his dwelling place (vs. 2). The lament shifts to a new
key, as God is addressed as King in hymnic tones:

Yet God my King is from of old,
  working salvation in the midst of the earth.
Thou didst divide the Sea [*Yam*] by thy might;
  thou didst break the heads of the dragons [*tanninim*] on the waters.
Thou didst crush the heads of Leviathan,
  thou didst give him as food for the creatures of the wilderness.[45]
Thou didst cleave open springs and brooks;
  thou didst dry up ever-flowing streams.
Thine is the day, thine also the night;
  thou hast established the luminaries and the sun.
Thou hast fixed all the bounds of the earth;
  thou hast made summer and winter.
                    —PSALM 74:12–17

Here there are distinct allusions to the myth—known especially
from Ugaritic texts—of the god who slays Leviathan (Ugaritic:
Lothan), the dragon with seven heads.[46] Clearly the psalmist
intends to extol the Creator, who has demonstrated his power
over chaos by cleaving open springs and brooks and drying up
the "ever-flowing rivers" (*neharoth 'ethan;* cf. Ps. 104:10). How-

[45] The translation "for the creatures of the wilderness" is uncertain.
The Hebrew has this: "for the people, for the dwellers of the wilderness
[?]." Later the view arose that Leviathan would be food for the Messianic
banquet; cf. Apocalypse of Baruch 29:4.
[46] Perhaps "dragons" in vs. 13 should be singular: "Dragon." See Isa.
27:1, which will be discussed in Chap. 4. Cyrus H. Gordon stresses the rela-

ever, the connection of this mythical symbolism with Israel's *Heilsgeschichte* is not so clear as in Psalm 77, which we have considered above. Crucial for interpretation is verse 12, and especially the clause translated "working salvation [Hebrew: "doing deeds of salvation"] in the midst of the earth." Does this refer to the divine deeds at the beginning when, according to the creation myth, the monster of chaos was slain? Or does the psalmist allude to Israel's *Urzeit*, when Yahweh delivered his people by "dividing" or "drying up" (vss. 13a, 15b) the sea? In the last analysis we are not forced to choose between these sharp alternatives, for the psalmist's use of creation imagery carries overtones from Israel's historical experience: the victory at the Reed Sea, the crossing of the Jordan, and the entry into the Promised Land.[47] When one considers these hymnic verses in the context of the psalm as a whole, the psalmist's concern is unmistakably historical: to express "the unshakable belief that God, who has shown himself in the creation of the universe to be Lord over the chaos, has now also the power to suppress the revolt of the chaotic powers." [48]

This historicizing of a mythical motif, which was probably accomplished within the Jerusalem cult, was carried out completely by Second Isaiah. Recalling the old myth of creation, he appeals to Yahweh to arouse himself "as in days of old" when the sea dragon Rahab was slain and the sea was dried up. That time of Yahweh's creative action, says the prophet, was the historical time when Yahweh created his people: when he

---

tion of these passages to Ugaritic mythology in his essay "Leviathan: Symbol of Evil" [65].

[47] J. L. McKenzie [101] argues that in all probability "the phenomena described in Ps. 74:13–15 are creative works, and not the historical events of the Exodus; and that the imagery employed is derived from Semitic—principally Canaanite—mythology." On the other hand, Samuel Terrien maintains [146] that vs. 12 "alludes to the Exodus and the other *Gesta Dei* which Israel remembered as the basis of its historical existence." He continues: "these deeds of salvation are performed continuously throughout history 'at the center of the earth' "—a phrase which he takes to refer to the view that the temple was situated over the "navel" of the earth. The commentaries by A. Weiser [154] and H. J. Kraus [92] stress the blending of creation traditions and historical traditions.

[48] Weiser, *The Psalms* [154], p. 520.

cut a path through the Great Deep (i.e. the Reed Sea) in order
that the redeemed could pass over. And it was a typological
anticipation of the New Creation, when Yahweh would make
a path through the chaotic waters so that his people could
pass over into the Promised Land of his purpose:

> Awake, awake, put on strength,
>> O arm of Yahweh;
> awake, as in days of old,
>> the generations of long ago.
> Was it not thou that didst cut Rahab in pieces,
>> that didst pierce the dragon [*tannin*]?
> Was it not thou that didst dry up Sea [*Yam*],
>> the waters of the great deep [*Tehom Rabbah*];
> that didst make the depths of the sea a way
>> for the redeemed to pass over?
> And the ransomed of Yahweh shall return,
>> and come with singing to Zion;
> everlasting joy shall be upon their heads;
>> they shall obtain joy and gladness,
>> and sorrow and sighing shall flee away.
>> —ISAIAH 51:9–11

If it was within the cult that the cosmological myth was historicized to refer to Yahweh's victory when he created Israel
to be his people, it was also in the same setting of worship that
Israel caught the vision of Yahweh's eschatological kingdom—
the Day of Yahweh when all the powers of death and darkness
would be vanquished and Yahweh's lordship would be un-
challenged by any enemy, historical or cosmic. We stand here
on the threshold of the understanding that creation has an
eschatological dimension. Men may put their trust in life's
meaning in spite of the chaotic threats of history because the
whole historical drama, from beginning to end, is enfolded
within the purpose of the God who is worshiped as creator and
redeemer. The full implications of this became increasingly
apparent when the theme of Yahweh's kingship over the rebellious waters of chaos was transposed out of the cult into the
language of prophecy and apocalyptic.

CHAPTER

4

Creation and Consummation

IN THE BIBLE creation opens toward the horizon of the future. Time rather than space, history rather than cosmology is the central concern. It is not accidental that the Christian Bible moves from the book of Genesis to the Apocalypse of John, from creation to the vision of "the new heaven and the new earth." Creation and consummation, first things and last things, are inseparably joined together, like Siamese twins. The first words of the Bible, "in the beginning," have as their counterpart the prophetic expectation, "in the end." Ludwig Köhler rightly observes that creation is an eschatological belief.

> To the beginning there corresponds an ending, to creation a completion, to the "very good" here the "perfect" yonder; they correpond, each to each; in the theology of the Old Testament creation is an eschatological conception.[1]

I

One does not have to resort to exegetical tricks to show that this eschatological orientation is already implicit in the first

---

[1] *Old Testament Theology* [89], p. 71. See also Edmund Jacob, *Theology of the Old Testament* [81], pp. 141 f.

chapter of Genesis. According to an interpretation of the Hebrew which is as old as the Greek Septuagint, a translation
begun in the third century B.C., the Hebrew book of Genesis
opens with an absolute statement: "In the beginning God
created the heavens and the earth." Admittedly, it is grammat-
ically possible to translate the Hebrew text as a temporal clause
which leads up to the main affirmation in vs. 3, in which case
the translation would run: "When God began to create the
heavens and the earth, the earth being without form and void
. . . God said, 'Let there be light' and there was light." [2] In this
case, the formulation would be like other ancient creation
stories, such as the Yahwist account which begins "In the day
that Yahweh God made the earth and the heavens . . ." (Gen.
2:4b–7) or the Babylonian creation epic which opens with
"When on high the heavens had not been named. . . ." Although this view has marshalled impressive support, beginning
with the medieval Jewish scholar Rashi, it poses exegetical
difficulties. Chief of these is the problem that the Priestly
writer, who intends to stress the transcendence of God as the
sole source of all that is, would be adopting the ancient mythical view of a preexistent chaos, independent of God. It is
therefore best to follow the Septuagint and to read Genesis 1:1
as a complete sentence, a reading which is as defensible gram-
matically as the translation which makes it part of a temporal
clause.[3] According to this reading, the word "beginning"
(re'shith) indicates an absolute temporal beginning, as Walther
Eichrodt has persuasively argued, and it implies the counterpart of the "end" ('aharith), as in the prophecy of Second

---

[2] See the translation in *The Old Testament: An American Translation*
(University of Chicago Press, 1927) ; *The Torah: The Five Books of Moses*
(Jewish Publication Society of America, 1962) ; also E. A. Speiser's trans-
lation in The Anchor Bible: *Genesis* [142].

[3] See the judicious discussion of Gen. 1:1–3 by Brevard Childs in *Myth
and Reality in the Old Testament* [27], pp. 30–42. He shows how in these
verses a tension exists between biblical and pagan views of reality and
how the Priestly writer, by making Gen. 1:1 an independent affirmation,
"has broken the myth," though not destroying it altogether.

Isaiah where "first" and "last" are juxtaposed (Isa. 44:6; 48:12).[4]

Moreover, the eschatological outlook of the Priestly creation story is evidenced in a major concern which runs through the entire account: the creation and ordering of time. It is theologically significant that the creation of light (day) took place before the creation of the luminaries: the sun, moon, and stars (cf. Gen. 1:3-5 with 1:14-19). Here the issue is not whether these bodies are a source of light (as any observer, ancient or modern, would know), but whether they are the source of time and therefore justify the astrologer's attempt to divine man's future fate on the basis of their movements. The *Enuma elish* myth, it will be recalled, attached much importance to Marduk's seizure of the Tablets of Fate from the rebel forces of chaos. In Babylonian and Assyrian culture an extraordinary accuracy in the study of the heavenly bodies was achieved, but this astronomical observation was based on the belief that the movement of the heavenly bodies disclosed omens of the fate of mankind which the gods had determined. According to the Priestly view, however, these luminaries are appointed to a particular task: to mark the times and the seasons. They are merely servants of the God who is the creator of the times, the inaugurator of history. The times are in his hand, filled with the content of his purpose, and directed toward the outcome he has in view. "The beginning," writes James Muilenburg, "was the creation of the first day (Gen. 1:1-5); the end will be the last day"—the Day "when God will assert his rule over all that he has created." [5] The Priestly writer's interest in time is also shown by the way he compresses the earlier tradition of

---

4 Walther Eichrodt, "In the Beginning" [39]. See also E. Jacob (*Theology of the Old Testament* [81], pp. 138 f.) : "For Israel creation marks a commencement. The word *re'shith* (Gen. 1:1) is a whole plan of action, because it shows us that God's plan in history has created its starting point."

5 James Muilenburg, *The Way of Israel* [112], Chap. 6 on "The Way of the Future," quoted from p. 129. Note also the observation by B. Childs ([27], p. 39) : "In the cyclic thinking of astrology, time has no particular significance. It is only when a *history* is established that the marking of a progression achieves importance."

eight creative acts (days) into the structure of a week—six days of work culminating in the Sabbath Rest.[6] This he was able to do by assigning two creative acts to the third day (vss. 9–13) and two to the sixth (vss. 24–31).

These remarks about Genesis 1 are more than ever to the point if, as suggested in the previous chapter, the Priestly creation story presupposes the Jerusalem cult and was even used liturgically in the fall festival at the turn of the year. The Jerusalem cult, as we have seen, gave special prominence to Yahweh's cosmic and universal kingship. In Jerusalem Yahweh's cosmic rule was not just accepted as an article of faith; it was a cultic experience in the temple festival when Yahweh, "the King of Glory," entered into Zion. The hymns of Yahweh's kingship, the so-called "Enthronement Psalms," (see above, pp. 99–102), glorify Yahweh for his action as creator in founding the world and in pushing back the rebellious powers of chaos, so that in place of darkness and confusion there is an ordered world of light and meaning. However one understands the "cultic drama" of the Jerusalem temple, one thing is clear: belief in Yahweh as creator belonged within the context of the anticipation of Yahweh's coming to overthrow his enemies, to judge the nations, and to establish his kingly rule.

> Say among the nations, "Yahweh reigns! [or, "Yahweh is King!"]
>   Yea, the world is established, it shall never be moved;
>   he will judge the peoples with equity."
> Let the heavens be glad, and let the earth rejoice;
>   let the sea roar, and all that fills it;
>   let the field exult, and everything in it!
> Then shall all the trees of the wood sing for joy
>   before Yahweh, for he comes,
>   for he comes to judge the earth.
> He will judge the world with righteousness,
>   and the peoples with his truth.
>   —PSALM 96:10–13

---

6 On the eschatological implications of the Sabbath Rest (cf. Heb. 3:1–4:13), see Gerhard von Rad's essay in *The Problem of the Hexateuch and Other Essays* [123], pp. 94–102.

If this psalm was used in connection with Israel's New Year festival, it indicates that worship was infused with a profound historical consciousness—a joyful anticipation of the Day when Yahweh would fulfill his purpose in history. The faith which remembers God's creative action in the beginning also looks forward to the finishing of his work at the completion of the historical drama. Unlike other cults of the ancient Near East, Israelites did not merely look forward to a "cultic day" which marked the turning point in the great annual cycle of nature. Rather, as R. E. Clements observes, "the Day of Yahweh which was celebrated in Israel's New Year Festival was thought to point forward to the day when Yahweh would carry to completion his purposes for his people." [7]

II

Throughout this study I have emphasized that in the Bible the creation-faith expresses Israel's understanding of history. Creation is primarily a category of history, not of nature; therefore it is wrong to regard the creation account as an explanation of the universe, that is, a cosmogony which belongs in the sphere of natural science. There is no clearer evidence that creation is to be understood in relation to history than the biblical portrayal of the consummation of history as the "new creation." On the assumption that a historical correspondence exists between the beginning and the end, Israel portrays the goal of the historical drama in the imagery of the starting point. The last things correspond to the first things.

In his study of *Creation and Chaos*, to which we have turned numerous times, Gunkel expressed this correspondence in his famous formula, *Urzeit gleich Endzeit* ("beginning-time equals end-time"). He ventured to say that Israel's thinking was pro-

---

[7] *Prophecy and Covenant* [29], p. 108; all of Chap. VI is illuminating in this connection. See also John Gray, *The Legacy of Canaan* ([66], pp. 91–92), who maintains that while "the kingship of Baal was menaced by the same chaotic forces with calendrical regularity," in Israel the theme of the triumph over chaos in the New Year festival became the basis for "projecting her faith into the future, not as a recurring cycle, but as a progressive development."

foundly influenced by the mythical view of time, which *equates* beginning and end. So before turning to Second Isaiah, who understands Israel's historical calling and destiny between the eschatological horizons of beginning and end, it is appropriate to consider briefly the meaning of this correspondence in a mythical context of thinking.

Most westerners think of Time as an impersonal process, spelled with a capital "T," which inexorably moves on under the tyranny of the clock. This chronological process, which can be analyzed mathematically into seconds, minutes, hours, days, weeks, months, and years, we liken to a mighty river, as in the well-known hymn:

> Time like an ever-rolling stream
> Bears all its sons away.
> They fly forgotten as the dream
> fades at the break of day.

Ancient man, however, spoke of "times" in the plural, that is, a sequence of times *(kairoi)*, each of which had a definite content. In this way of thinking the purpose of a calendar was not to measure time mathematically, as with us, but rather to indicate the sacred times, the festivals, which bring man in relation to the Great Time from which, like a fountain, the times well up. The *Endzeit,* according to this view, is not just "like" the *Urzeit;* the two are identical. The *Endzeit* has the same content as that primal Time which arose at the beginning, and therefore it is the same time. Through cultic celebration man returns to the beginning; he participates sacramentally in a repetition of the primordial creation of order out of chaos "in days of old." Therefore, there is no temporal progression but only *timelessness.*

> The mythical consciousness tends to allow time "to stand still"; this means however not that the clock stands still, but that every "when" has become a matter of sheer indifference. It is in this time-lessness that *fairy tales* subsist: in an eternal present, or "in those days," or "once upon a time." [8]

---

[8] G. van der Leeuw, *Religion in Essence and Manifestation* [96], p. 385. Cf. Childs, *Myth and Reality* [27], pp. 72 ff.

If we may speak of this time-consciousness as a fountain springing up from a primeval act of creation, in which past, present,
and future are not separated, it should be added that this
fountain is like a geyser—an "Old Faithful"—which springs up
periodically at certain sacred places and in response to cultic
reenactment.[9]

The mention of sacred places introduces another dimension
of typology which was characteristic of religions of the ancient
Near East: not the correspondence which exists on a horizontal plane but that which exists on a vertical plane. Ancient
man believed that the ordered structure of the universe—
heaven, earth, and underearth—was evident in the fact that
things terrestrial are replicas or copies of their heavenly pro-
totypes. The temple on earth, for instance, was thought to be
a copy of the deity's heavenly Temple, and even cities of Babylon were thought to have their pattern in certain constellations.[10] Worshipers who participated cultically in the repetition of creation thought it necessary to be at the Center—
whether it was a sacred mountain, a sacred city, or a temple
(e.g. the ziggurat)—for this was held to be "the meeting point
of heaven, earth, and hell" and "the point at which creation
began." [11] For instance, Babylon, sometimes called "Bond of
Heaven and Earth," or "House of the Base of Heaven and
Earth," was thought to be built upon "the Gate of the Apsu,"
i.e. the waters of chaos upon which the earth was founded at
creation. Or in Egypt, as we have seen (on pp. 45–58), it was believed that a temple was built on the primeval hill which arose
out of the waters of the abyss, the very hill on which Amon-Re
began his creation. In building a temple it was important to
find "a position where Power resided," for from time imme-
morial men have made pilgrimages to those places "where the
Power of the universe renewed itself daily, and where the
heart of the world could be approached." [12]

---

[9] See van der Leeuw's discussion of the calendar and the sacred festivals
[96], Chaps. 55 and 56. Also Mircea Eliade, *The Sacred and the Profane*
[45], especially Chaps. I and II.

[10] See M. Eliade, *Cosmos and History* [44], pp. 6 ff.

[11] Eliade [44], pp. 12 ff.

[12] Van der Leeuw [96], pp. 400, 401.

Thus typologies of space and time blended together in the religions of the ancient world: on the one hand a typology which portrayed a correspondence between the macrocosm and the microcosm, the celestial and the terrestrial; and on the other hand, a typology which depicted a correspondence between the first and the last, *Urzeit* and *Endzeit*. Of these two typologies, the vertical typology exerted a specially strong influence upon the Jerusalem cultic tradition, and to some extent the influence was felt in prophetic and apocalyptic literature. The Priestly tradition of the Pentateuch, for instance, preserves the idea that the tabernacle is to be built according to its celestial prototype. On Mount Sinai, Yahweh shows Moses the "pattern" *(tabnith)* for the sacred tabernacle and all its sacred equipment.

"According to all that I show you concerning the pattern of the tabernacle, and of all its furniture, so you shall make it."
—Exodus 25:9; cf. vs. 40

Doubtless this passage reflects the view which prevailed in the Jerusalem cult: that the Jerusalem temple was built according to the model of Yahweh's cosmic house (cf. Ezek. 40:1–4). Furthermore, it was believed that the Jerusalem temple was located at the Center. Accordingly, Ezekiel 47:1–12 conceives of the temple as built at the "navel" (cf. Ezek. 38:12) of the earth, for in the vision a stream of water issues from below the threshold of the temple, having its source in the waters under the earth, and flows in a life-giving stream through the Judean wilderness to the Dead Sea. The psalmist's praise of God for "doing his deeds of deliverance at the center of the earth" (Ps. 74:12) may reflect the view that the Jerusalem temple was located at the *omphalos* of the earth, where Israel remembered the Exodus and the other historical deeds of God [13] (see discussion of Ps. 74 above, pp. 107 f.). And to take one more example, Jerusalem was believed to be built upon a mountain identical with the great Mountain at the center of the earth to

---

13 So Samuel Terrien, "Creation, Cultus, and Faith in the Psalter" [146], p. 119. See his references to further studies of "the navel of the earth" on p. 126, n. 19.

which all peoples will ultimately make pilgrimage (Isa. 2:2–4; Mic. 4:1–4). Indeed, it was equated with the Olympus of Canaanite mythology: Mount Zaphon in the far north (the imposing 3,000-foot Mount Casius or *jebel 'el-'akra'* on the coast of Syria) where the divine abode was supposedly located (see Ps. 48:3). Yet even the Jerusalem cult, with its strong interest in these mythological notions, broke with the pagan view at the crucial point: Yahweh did not establish Zion as his dwelling place in the *Urzeit,* the primeval time; rather, he *chose* Zion in connection with the historical events of David's career. The holiness of Jerusalem was based on Yahweh's historical action, not on the primal power released at creation.[14]

However, the "vertical" correspondence between celestial and terrestrial, or "up" and "down," was not as serviceable to the faith of Israel as the "horizontal" correspondence between *Urzeit* and *Endzeit.* Apparently the people of Israel were not as interested in the spatial dimension as modern people who have become excited about Bishop J. A. T. Robinson's widely read paperback, *Honest to God,* which boldly challenges beliefs supposedly based on the so-called three-storied view of the universe. The axis of Israel's faith was not cosmology (space) but history (time). Hence the *Urzeit-Endzeit* correspondence became increasingly important in prophecy and eventually in apocalyptic, though this typology was profoundly modified according to the historical demands of Israel's faith. In Israel the *Urzeit* was freed from the mythical pattern of cultic repetition, a pattern which allowed no room for what was historically new and unique, and it became the commencement of a movement in history. The phenomenologist G. van der Leeuw observes that "one of the most important dates in the history of religion" occurred when Israel transposed the old nature festivals into *"commemorations* of historical dates, which were simultaneously manifestations of power and deeds of God." This happened, for instance, when the old spring festival of Passover was changed into a festival celebrating the

---

14 Childs [27], pp. 82–93, especially pp. 88–91.

deliverance from Egypt. "Something completely new," he points out, "was inaugurated."

> The notch in time is then no longer repeatable at will; duration is no longer entirely swallowed up in the festal cycle: God Himself makes the notch once for all: He arrests time and transforms the mere given into a promise.[15]

This historical typology, which allows for dynamic movement in history and the appearance of that which is radically new, is basic to the prophecy of Second Isaiah. In the message of this prophet of the Exile Israel's creation-faith comes to its finest and maturest expression in the Old Testament.

III

There are striking affinities between the Yahwist and Second Isaiah. Both interpreters of Israel's faith are anonymous; their historical individuality is a discovery of modern scholarly research. But even more important is the similarity of the historical situation in which each attempted a reinterpretation of Israel's faith. In some respects that situation was like our own time when many people find that the cultic life and institutional forms of the church have lost their meaning. The Yahwist's epic was composed at a time when Israel was pushed out of the cultic sphere of the Tribal Confederacy into the political arena, where under the leadership of David and Solomon, Israel became a state. In that situation the Yahwist's inclusion of the *Urgeschichte,* in which creation is portrayed as the beginning of history, boldly emphasized Yahweh's sovereignty in *the secular sphere* (see above, pp. 56–57). The Second Isaiah, likewise, inherited much from the cult, including the theme of the kingship of Yahweh which was prominent in the Jerusalem ceremonial of the New Year. But he lived in a time when the temple had been destroyed and the old Jerusalem cult had been discontinued. It is possible that Second Isaiah was among the exiles displaced from Jerusalem at the

---

15 Van der Leeuw [96], pp. 391 f.

time of the fall of the nation, and that the disintegration of the old cultic patterns provided the opportunity for him to restate the theological convictions which had once been nourished in the cult.[16] This is conjectural in the nature of the case. It is incontestable, however, that the poetic prophecy found in Isaiah 40–55 is related in some way to the great hymns of the Psalter celebrating Yahweh's kingship. Second Isaiah's prophecy expands the creation-faith expressed in these hymns into a theology of world history, in which Yahweh's salvation is his gracious answer to the problem of human existence as such.

Strikingly, not once does Second Isaiah deal with creation by itself, apart from history.[17] In one cluster of passages creation is invoked as a demonstration of Yahweh's cosmic wisdom and power and therefore as an assurance that he is able to save. (Compare the psalms with a soteriological interest, discussed above, pp. 93–99.) This is the case in Isaiah 40 where the prophet addresses a people who, in despair, suppose that they have been deserted by their God and that history is meaningless:

Have you not known? Have you not heard?
    Has it not been told you from the beginning?
    Have you not understood from the foundations of the earth?
It is he who sits above the circle of the earth,
    and its inhabitants are like grasshoppers;
who stretches out the heavens like a curtain,
    and spreads them like a tent to dwell in;
who brings princes to nought,
    and makes the rulers of the earth as nothing.
                                        —ISAIAH 40:21–23

Like the writer of the Eighth Psalm, the prophet overwhelms his hearers with the incredible good news that the God who assigns the stars their function and who holds the whole uni-

---

[16] Cf. R. E. Clements, *Prophecy and Covenant* [29], pp. 116 f.

[17] Cf. G. von Rad, "The Theological Problem of the Creation-faith" in *Essays* [123], pp. 131–43. See also J. Muilenburg's commentary on Isaiah 40–66 in *The Interpreter's Bible* [2], Vol. V, pp. 318–419.

verse in his grasp is mindful of his puny people, whose life is as frail as the flower of the field. This God, he says, cannot be compared to anything in nature or in history, for he is neither a natural power nor a historical phenomenon: he is God absolutely.

> To whom then will you compare me,
>   that I should be like him? says the Holy One.
> Lift up your eyes on high and see:
>   who created these?
> He who brings out their host by number,
>   calling them all by name;
> by the greatness of his might,
>   and because he is strong in power
>   not one is missing.
>   —ISAIAH 40:25–26

The trouble with idols—whether the gods of nature represented in wood and stone or the "causes" and "values" which man creates—is that they wear out. Like man, they get tired. They cannot sustain man, who from birth to death is restless with an "ontological thirst"—a thirst to find out who he really is, to discover what life is really about. Second Isaiah bears witness to the tireless God whose inexhaustible strength and grace can overcome man's fatigue with life. For, he says, Yahweh is the creator of the ends of the earth, who does not grow weary and whose understanding is unfathomable. He alone is worthy of absolute trust.

> Even youths shall faint and be weary,
>   and young men shall fall exhausted;
> but they who wait for Yahweh shall renew their strength,
>   they shall mount up with wings like eagles,
> they shall run and not be weary,
>   they shall walk and not faint.
>   —ISAIAH 40:30–31

Second Isaiah, however, does not think of creation *only* in terms of Yahweh's absolute lordship and the dependence of every creature upon his sovereign will. Rather, he thinks of creation as an absolute temporal beginning (as in Gen. 1:1), when

God created the heavens and the earth. This is clear, as Walther Eichrodt has shown, in Isaiah 40:21, where the expression
"from the beginning" stands in parallelism with "from the
foundations of the earth." [18]

> Has it not been told you from the beginning [*re'shith*]?
> Have you not understood from the foundations of the earth?

The thought of creation as the absolute beginning of history
prompts the prophet to contemplate in awe the eternity of God
who reigns in transcendent majesty above history and therefore commands the entire human drama from beginning to
end. The idols of the nations are bound within the cycle of
nature: they cannot declare a historical purpose and bring it to
realization. And man is a transient creature who, unable to
grasp the meaning of the whole of history, is driven to the
silly manufacture of idols. But Yahweh, who is the first even
as he is the last (41:4), comprehends the entire succession of
events from beginning to end, just as a musician hears successive notes as a melody. Therefore to the prophet the triumph
of Cyrus was not a chance development; it occurred within the
plan of the eternal God who called the generations from the
very beginning.

> Thus says Yahweh, the King of Israel
>   and his Redeemer, the Lord of hosts:
> "I am the first and I am the last;
>   besides me there is no god.
> Who is like me? Let him proclaim it,
>   let him declare and set it forth before me.
> Who has announced from of old the things to come?
>   Let them tell us what is yet to be.
> Fear not, nor be afraid;
>   have I not told you from of old and declared it?
>   And you are my witnesses!
> Is there a God besides me?
>   There is no Rock; I know not any."
>   —ISAIAH 44:6–8

---

[18] See W. Eichrodt's essay, "In the Beginning" [39].

Belief in creation is not an adornment of this prophetic message but rather its very substance. The salvation of Israel and of mankind is—according to Second Isaiah—firmly anchored in the purpose of the Eternal God, the Creator, who has made known the end from the beginning.

It is striking, however, that in the message of Second Isaiah creation is not limited to the absolute temporal beginning. Not only is creation a historical commencement but, as Carroll Stuhlmueller observes, "history is a continuation of this creative power of God." [19] In Second Isaiah's prophecy creation is a broad conception which includes all God's saving actions, from the beginning of history to its consummation, as can be seen from the list of creation-verbs in the table on pp. 124–26. Notice that special emphasis is given to the verb *bara'*, the verb which is used only of God's creative action (never of man's creativity!) and which takes for its object the product of God's act, rather than material. Since this verb indicates the uniqueness of God's action, it is significant that it occurs in Second Isaiah more than any other place in the Old Testament.[20] But in Second Isaiah's poems even the verb *yatzar*, which is based on the image of the potter working with clay (Gen. 1:7), and the verb *'asah*, which conveys the idea of making something out of material (like a carpenter), also express Yahweh's absolute sovereignty (see, for instance, 45:9–13). In this respect, the situation is similar to the Priestly creation story where the

---

[19] Carroll Stuhlmueller, C. P., "The Theology of Creation in Second Isaias" [145], p. 435. See also R. Rendtorff, "Die theologische Stellung des Schöpfungsglaubens bei Deuterojesaja" [128].

[20] *Bara'* occurs in P in Gen. 1:1; 2:3, 4 (heavens and earth); 1:27; 5:1–2 (mankind); 1:21 (sea creatures). Besides these occurrences and those listed in the table on pp. 124–26, the verb occurs in Gen. 6:7 [J]; Deut. 4:32; Ps. 89:48 (mankind); Ps. 141:5 (heavens); Ps. 104:30 (creatures); Ps. 89:12 (north and south); Amos 4:13 (the wind); Mal. 2:11; Eccles. 12:1 (the individual); Ps. 102:18 (a generation of people); Ezek. 21:30 (the people Ammon); 28:13, 15 (king of Tyre); Isa. 4:5 (cloud and flame); Ex. 34:10; Num. 16:30 [J]; Jer. 31:22 (miracles); also, a "clean heart" (Ps. 51:12). See the study by Paul Humbert, "Emploi et portée du verbe *bārā* [créer] dans l'Ancien Testament" [79].

verbs "create" *(bara')* and "make" *('asah)* are used interchangeably in the present form of the story.[21]

VERBS OF CREATION IN SECOND ISAIAH

Of the various verbs of creation used by Second Isaiah, this table concentrates on only the three which appear prominently in the two creation stories, that of the Priestly writer (Gen. 1:1–2:4a) and the Yahwist (Gen. 2:4b–25). The three chief verbs are: *bara'* ("create," always used of God's creative activity for which there is no human analogy), *'asah* ("make," often used of man's construction of something), and *yatzar* ("form," presupposing the analogy of the potter molding clay).

Note: in the table "ptcp" = "participle."

	bara'	*'asah*	*yatzar*
1. *Primordial deeds*			
The heavenly host	40:26		
Creator of the ends of the earth	40:28 (ptcp)		
Created the heavens and stretched them out (parallel to "spread out [*raqa'*] the earth)	42:5 (ptcp)		
Made all things (parallel to "stretched out the heavens" and "spread out [*raqa'*] the earth")		44:24 (ptcp)	
Made the earth, created man (parallel to "stretched out the heavens," "commanded their host")	45:12	45:12	

---

21 The Priestly account, however, is the end-product of a long history of liturgical usage. In the earliest stage the story may have regarded God as "Maker" (e.g. Gen. 1:7) ; at a more sophisticated stage he was regarded as "Creator" by fiat (e.g. 1:6). In the history of tradition the two theological conceptions were blended in such a manner as to give the weight to creation by fiat.

	bara'	'asah	yatzar
Created the heavens,	45:18		
formed, made the earth,		45:18	45:18
(established [kun] it)			
did not create it a chaos,	45:18		
formed it to be inhabited			45:18

2. *Historical deeds*

Created the smith,	54:16		
created the ravager	54:16		
Created, formed Israel	43:1 (ptcp)		43:1 (ptcp)
Created, formed, made			
his people	43:7	43:7	43:7
The Creator of Israel	43:15 (ptcp)		
Israel, the people whom			
Yahweh formed for			
himself			43:21
Made Israel the servant,		44:2 (ptcp)	
formed him from the			
womb			44:2 (ptcp)
Formed Israel, the servant			44:21
Formed Israel from the			
womb			44:24 (ptcp)
Israel's Maker			45:11 (ptcp)
(cf. 45:9 for the image			
of potter in a more gen-			
eral sense)			
Yahweh has made Israel,		46:4	
borne him from birth			
Formed the Servant from			
the womb (cf. 49:1			49:5 (ptcp)
called from the womb)			
Israel's Maker		51:13 (ptcp)	
Israel's Maker		54:5 (ptcp)	

3. *Eschatological deeds*

The hand of Yahweh has		41:20	
done this, has created	41:20		
it (the New Exodus of			
salvation)			

	bara'	'asah	yatzar
He has performed the raising of Cyrus (parallel to "done" [pa'al])		41:4	
Forms light,			45:7
creates darkness;	45:7		
Makes weal,		45:7	
creates woe	45:7		
He creates the new age of salvation	45:8		
He creates the "new things" (cf. He does [makes] a new thing)	48:7	(43:19)	
He creates the healing which issues from repentance ("the fruit of the lips")	57:18		
New heavens and new earth *	65:17 (ptcp)		
Rejoice in what Yahweh creates,	65:18 (ptcp)		
for he creates a new Jerusalem	65:18 (ptcp)		

IV

However, of all Yahweh's creative acts—primordial, historical, and eschatological—Second Isaiah places special emphasis upon the creation of Israel. Yahweh is preeminently "Israel's Maker." Israel's history had its creative beginning in Yahweh's act.

> But now thus says Yahweh,
>> he who created [bara'] you, O Jacob,
>> he who formed [yatzar] you, O Israel:
> "Fear not, for I have redeemed you;
>> I have called you by name, you are mine."
>>> —ISAIAH 43:1

---

* Isa. 65:17–18 is usually held to come from the disciples of Second Isaiah (Trito-Isaiah) who here echo the theme of "the former things" and "the new things" (cf. Second Isaiah's treatment of this motif in 48:3–8).

Moreover, for Second Isaiah the time of Israel's creation was the time of the Exodus. When he thinks of Yahweh as the creator of Israel he calls to mind the events of the *Heilsgeschichte,* especially the great miracle of the sea, when Yahweh "made a way in the sea, a path in the mighty waters," when chariot and horse, army and warrior were overwhelmed—"extinguished, quenched like a wick" (Isa. 43:15–21). To be sure, in one passage, where the prophet apparently refers to the Priestly tradition concerning creation out of chaos (45:18–19), he affirms that it is not Yahweh's purpose to allow the earth to return to precreation chaos (*tohu;* cf. Jer. 4:23–26!); for although his "overflowing wrath" momentarily seemed to bring the threat of chaos (comparable to the Flood according to the P version), actually with "everlasting love" he binds himself to Israel with an unconditional covenant of grace, as in the days of Noah.

> "For this is like the days of Noah to me:
>   as I swore that the waters of Noah
>   should no more go over the earth,
> so I have sworn that I will not be angry with you
>   and will not rebuke you.
> For the mountains may depart
>   and the hills be removed,
> but my steadfast love [*ḥesed*] shall not depart from you,
>   and my covenant of peace shall not be removed,
>   says Yahweh, who has compassion on you."
>   —ISAIAH 54:9–10

By and large, however, this prophet does not employ chaos imagery in connection with the creation of the world; instead, he uses this imagery to portray the creation of Israel at the time of the Exodus. Yahweh's victory was not just against Pharaoh's armies, but against the powers of chaos. In early tradition the crossing of the Reed Sea was made possible when Yahweh intervened by using the forces of nature (the wind) on Israel's behalf.

> At the blast of thy nostrils the waters piled up,
>   the floods stood up in a heap;

the deeps congealed in the heart of the sea.
                                        —Exodus 15:8

According to this old hymn the sea was merely the passive instrument by which Yahweh won his victory.[22] But in Second
Isaiah's view the waters of the sea were none other than the
waters of chaos. Yahweh's battle was fought, not in the timeless realm of mythology, but in the arena of history—at the
historical beginning, when Israel was created to be his people.
It was then that Yahweh slew the monster Rahab, separated
the Great Deep (tehom rabbah) so that the people could pass
through (44:27), rebuked rebellious Sea (Yam; 51:10). Second
Isaiah's thought is precisely the same as in Psalm 77. Recalling
Yahweh's mighty deed of old when he redeemed his people,
the psalmist says:

> When the waters saw thee, O God,
>   when the waters saw thee, they were afraid,
>   yea, the deeps [tehomoth] trembled.
>   —Psalm 77:16

And, as the conclusion of the psalm indicates, the victory at
the Reed Sea is clearly in the poet's mind:

> Thy way was through the sea,
>   thy path through the great waters [mayim rabbim] . . .
>   —Psalm 77:19

Yet even in these contexts, where Second Isaiah portrays the
creation of Israel in mythological imagery, his thinking is
eschatological. He cannot dissociate Yahweh's past act of creation from the new act of creation which Yahweh is about to
perform. Hence the creation of Israel in the Exodus from
Egypt foreshadows the "New Exodus of salvation" when Yahweh will create something absolutely new. The correspondence
between the old Exodus and the new Exodus is a dominant
strain of Second Isaiah's prophecy.[23] Just as Yahweh was vic-

---

22 See above, pp. 37, 50, where this interpretation was advanced, against
scholars who believe, as does T. H. Gaster, that the myth of the defeat of
the sea dragon is present as "a kind of undertone," especially in vss. 8–10.
See his article "The Egyptian 'Story of Astarte' and the Ugaritic Poem of
Baal" [60], p. 82.
23 See my article "Exodus Typology in Second Isaiah" [14].

torious at the Reed Sea, driving back and conquering the waters of chaos, so in the time of the New Exodus he will show
his mighty arm against powers opposed to his purpose. In a
remarkable passage the prophet portrays Israel's deliverance
from the bondage of her exile and her guilt as Yahweh's new
victory over the Deep.

> Thus says Yahweh, your Redeemer,
>   who formed [yatzar] you from the womb:
> "I am Yahweh, who made ['asah] all things,
>   who stretched out the heavens alone,
>   who spread out the earth—Who was with me?—
> who frustrates the omens of liars,
>   and makes fools of diviners;
> who turns wise men back,
>   and makes their knowledge foolish;
> who confirms the word of his servant,
>   and performs the counsel of his messengers;
> who says of Jerusalem, 'She shall be inhabited,'
>   and of the cities of Judah, 'They shall be built,
>   and I will raise up their ruins';
> who says to the Deep [tzulah], 'Be dry,
>   I will dry up your rivers [neharoth]';
> who says of Cyrus, 'He is my shepherd,
>   and he shall fulfill all my purpose';
> saying of Jerusalem, 'She shall be built,'
>   and of the temple, 'Your foundation shall be laid.' "
>   —ISAIAH 44:24–28

The word translated "deep" (tzulah), which appears only here
in the Old Testament, is undoubtedly a reference to the watery
chaos; and the parallel term "rivers" (neharoth) refers here, as
elsewhere (e.g. Ps. 93:3–4; Hab. 3:8–15), to the rebellious waters.

In passages like these Second Isaiah understands the "New
Exodus of salvation" to be a new creation, comparable to the
event of the creation of Israel in the first Exodus. Yet while
the "new things"—the events of the New Exodus—correspond
to the "former things"—the events of the Heilsgeschichte,
chiefly the Exodus—they are not the same. The New Exodus
will be the climax of Yahweh's work and, in a profound sense,
something never heard of before:

> "From this time forth I make you hear new things,
>   hidden things which you have not known.
> They are created [*nibre'u,* from *bara'*] now, not long ago;
>   before today you have never heard of them,
>   lest you should say, 'Behold, I knew them.' "
>   —Isaiah 48:6b–7

With some reservation one may agree that Gunkel's formula, *Urzeit gleich Endzeit,* is applicable to the prophecy of Second Isaiah. There is a typological relationship between the beginning and the end, between creation and new creation. On the one hand, this typology involves *correspondence* of the events, for they are linked in the continuity of Yahweh's purpose. Hence the events which fulfill his historical purpose are understood to be related analogically to the events which initiate his purpose. On the other hand, there is an increase or enhancement *(Steigerung),* like the shift to a new key as music sweeps to a climax, for the new creation is not just the repetition of the original creation in a cyclical movement. The usage of the verb *bara'* (the verb expressing divine fiat) points to something radically new, unprecedented, unique. So, while the prophet could urge Israel in one breath to remember the "former things," he could say in the next that these things are no longer to be remembered, for Yahweh is about to create something startlingly new.

> "Remember not the former things,
>   nor consider the things of old,
> Behold, I am doing a new thing;
>   now it springs forth, do you not perceive it?"
>   —Isaiah 43:18–19a (cf. 42:9)

Second Isaiah was the herald of the good news which was proclaimed with christological meaning in the New Testament: ". . . the old has passed away, behold, the new has come" (II Cor. 5:17b).

In view of this twofold emphasis upon correspondence and difference, continuity and discontinuity, it is evident that Gunkel's formula, derived from ancient mythical views, breaks down at the crucial point not only in the prophecy of Second Isaiah but in Israel's faith as a whole. For this prophetic interpretation of history puts the accent on what is radically new, not upon a repetition of the creation drama.[24] Therefore, while the events of beginning and end are related analogically, they are not "equal" *(gleich)*—certainly not in the sense that *Urzeit* and *Endzeit* are identical in the mythical consciousness. And the most striking evidence of the decisive break with the mythical pattern is that creation symbolism is absorbed into Exodus symbolism, with the result that Israel's history is understood to be part of a historical drama which progresses from creation to new creation.

The heart of Second Isaiah's message, however, is the proclamation that the creation is happening *in the present* as Yahweh conquers the chaos of the Babylonian Exile and makes a path through the sea for his redeemed to pass over and return with singing to Jerusalem. Yahweh *is doing* (creating) a new thing. Even *now* it is springing forth. In the *present* his arm is outstretched to deliver. There can be no objection to speaking of this new creation as an "actualization" of the time of the Exodus if interpretation is kept free from the pagan conception of a *repetition* of the creative event, a *return* to the *Urzeit*. The prophet has taken creation completely out of the realm of mythology. For him creation is a historical event in the *now*. And from this historical standpoint he sees a series of redemptive acts, stretching back even before Israel's *Heilsgeschichte* to the beginning of time. Carroll Stuhlmueller's comment is pertinent:

> With ecstatic rapture he [Second Isaiah] finds himself witnessing God's power to create a new Jewish commonwealth out of the chaos of the Babylonian exile. This historical act of recreating Israel unveils God's power in creating the universe out of primal chaos.[25]

---

24 See Childs [27], pp. 77–80, who discerningly stresses the profound changes which Israel made in the mythical scheme. In view of these changes, it is questionable whether it is theologically proper to speak of the *Endzeit* as "a return to the *Urzeit*," as he does, for instance, on p. 80.

25 C. Stuhlmueller [145], p. 451.

V

So, Israelite prophets and poets appropriated the old chaos imagery in order to portray the continuing creative and redemptive work of God. The struggle between creation and chaos is one which goes on in the realm of history, and this historical struggle continues from the first day to the last day.[26] The raging, unruly waters of chaos symbolize the powers which threaten to destroy the meaningfulness of history, as though—to recall Jeremiah's vision—the world ever has the possibility of returning to chaos (Jer. 4:23–26). Creation continues, precisely because "at each moment of time, darkness must be dispelled and the raging waters of the abyss kept in their place by the creative word of God." [27]

Accordingly, it was believed that these demonic powers could manifest themselves in Israel's historical enemies. In ancient religions, it will be recalled, the identification of foes with the powers of chaos was prompted by the cultic repetition and actualization of the myth of the beginning. In Mesopotamian tradition, for instance, the historical catastrophe which destroyed Ur could be identified with the storm that raged at the origin of the world.[28] The role of the king in both Mesopotamian and Egyptian understanding was to destroy the enemies who incarnated the chaotic powers that threaten the order of creation. As we have seen in the previous chapter, similar claims were made within the Israelite cult in connection with the celebration of Yahweh's kingship. Thus Paul Humbert maintains that the book of Nahum, written in connection with the fall of the Assyrian capital Nineveh in 612 B.C., is the

---

26 "The fight which took place at the creation is, in a condensed form, that which is constantly occurring" (Johannes Pedersen, *Israel* [122], p. 472). See his brief discussion of how the chaos conception, which had its primary source in Mesopotamia, was appropriated by Israel (pp. 470–74).

27 Stuhlmueller [145], p. 465. On *creatio continua* see further Jacob, *Theology of the Old Testament* [81], pp. 139 f.

28 Thorkild Jacobsen, in *The Intellectual Adventure* [52], pp. 196–97. See also Paul Ricoeur, *The Symbolism of Evil* [132], Pt. II, Chap. I. For the identification of enemies with chaos powers in Egyptian thought, see Henri Frankfort, *Egyptian Religion* [54], p. 56.

prophet's interpretation of this event as Yahweh's triumph over the powers of chaos in the New Year festival. In Humbert's view the traditional imagery was laden with new historical meaning in that time: [29]

> His way is in whirlwind and storm,
>   and the clouds are the dust of his feet.
> He rebukes the sea and makes it dry,
>   he dries up all the rivers;
> Bashan and Carmel wither,
>   the bloom of Lebanon fades.
> The mountains quake before him,
>   the hills melt;
> the earth is laid waste before him,
>   the world and all that dwell therein.
>   —NAHUM 1:3b–5

In any case, the cult provided Israel's poets and prophets with metaphorical language for interpreting the meaning of historical crises. The "many waters" are sometimes equivalent to the "many peoples" who threaten Israel's existence and who are held by Yahweh within the bounds of his sovereign purpose.[30] A good illustration is this poem:

> Ah, the thunder of many peoples,
>   they thunder like the thundering of the sea!
> Ah, the roar of nations,
>   they roar like the roaring of mighty waters [*mayim rabbim*]!
> The nations roar like the roaring of many waters,
>   but he will rebuke them, and they will flee far away,
> chased like chaff on the mountains before the wind
>   and whirling dust before the storm.
> At evening time, behold, terror!
>   Before morning, they are no more!
> This is the portion of those who despoil us,
>   and the lot of those who plunder us.
>   —ISAIAH 17:12–14

---

29 P. Humbert, "Le problème du livre de Nahoum" [77].
30 See H. G. May, "Some Cosmic Implications of *Mayim Rabbim*" [100], especially pp. 11 f.

The repeated use of *like* clearly indicates that here the language has become poetic symbolism. Similarly, the Egyptian Pharaoh is said to be "like a dragon in the seas," whom Yahweh captures with his net, along with a host of "many peoples" (Ezek. 32:2 ff.).[31] Or of the people from the north it is said: ". . . the sound of them is like the roaring sea" (Jer. 6:22–23; cf. Jer. 50:41–42). In these instances poets draw upon mythological language to express a dimension of historical evil which posed a threat to Yahweh's historical purpose.

In apocalyptic literature the chaos imagery is developed further, though without reference to the typology of the Exodus and the New Exodus found classically in Second Isaiah. Since the sea symbolizes chaotic, demonic powers that were subdued by the Creator but not finally vanquished, apocalyptic writers looked to the future when the history-long conflict would be brought to an end. At that time the chaos monster, who was defeated and chained at the beginning, would break loose from his fetters and, making his last challenge, would be decisively overcome. According to a passage in "The Little Apocalypse" of Isaiah, the fate of Leviathan, whose uncanny power is felt in the conflicts of history, is sure:

> In that day Yahweh with his hard and great and strong hand will punish Leviathan the fleeing serpent, Leviathan the twisting serpent, and he will slay the dragon [*tannin*] that is in the sea.
>
> —ISAIAH 27:1 (cf. Ps. 74:12–19)

The similarity of this passage to the Ugaritic myth of Baal's victory over Leviathan *(Ltn)* the "Primeval Serpent" is remarkable. The similarity extends even to language.

> Though thou didst smite Ltn the Primaeval Serpent,[32]

---

[31] A couple of Hebrew manuscripts read *tannin* (rather than *tannim*), which would make the comparison even closer with Ras Shamra texts which speak of Leviathan as *tnn*. Cf. May [100], p. 15. He also discusses other passages, like Ezek. 26:19 (Tyre) and 31:15 (Egypt) in which the language of chaos—i.e. *Tehom*, "many waters," sea—is used to express the judgment of God in history.

[32] Translation according to J. Gray, *The Legacy of Canaan* ([66], pp. 30 f.). Following W. F. Albright, he translates *ltn btn brh* as Ltn (Levia-

> And didst annihilate the Crooked Serpent [same as "twisting
>   serpent," Isa. 27:1],
> The Close-coiling One of Seven Heads,
> The heavens will dry up, yea, languish;
> I shall pound thee, consume thee, and eat thee,
> Cleft, forspent, and exhausted.
> Thou shalt indeed go down into the throat of Mot the son
>   of El.

According to the apocalyptic writer of Isaiah 27:1, Yahweh's victory in the *Endzeit* will be a final victory over the enemy defeated in the *Urzeit*.

This *Urzeit-Endzeit* ("beginning-time–end-time") formulation, which apocalyptic writers inherited from prophecy, has been challenged by Rudolf Bultmann because, in his view, it reflects a non-prophetic (non-biblical) view of history.[33] On this ground he argues against typology as a hermeneutical method and in favor of the New Testament motif of the fulfillment of prophecy. According to him, these two approaches— typology and prophecy—presuppose different conceptions of time and history. The appeal to prophecy rests upon the genuine Old Testament view of *Heilsgeschichte,* a sacred history which God directs to its fulfillment. But typology (the portrayal of the end-time in the imagery of the beginning-time) allegedly lacks a genuine understanding of history. It presupposes the cosmological idea of the cyclical movement of world periods by repetition and the return of the same events *(die Wiederkehr des Gleichens)*—an idea found in both Greece and the ancient Orient. This view, he says, found its way into Israel through the New Year festival, when worshipers actualized the *Heilszeit* ("time of salvation") and thus participated in the cosmic renewal of the universe. He admits that Israel made

---

than) "the Primaeval Serpent," instead of "the fleeing serpent." The exact phrase appears in Isa. 27:1 and Job 26:23. See also Ps. 74:12 ff., which refers to Yahweh crushing the heads of Leviathan. Similar statements are made regarding the dragon Rahab in Isa. 51:9 ff. and Ps. 89:6–18. Rahab, however, is not mentioned in Ugaritic texts.

[33] See his article "Ursprung und Sinn der Typologie als hermeneutischer Methode" [24].

modifications in the mythical pattern. Nevertheless, he contends, the hope for the return of the glorious *Urzeit* is fundamentally at odds with the prophetic interpretation of history.

Here we cannot go into the whole question of typology as a hermeneutical key to the understanding of the relation between the Testaments.[34] But we may ask whether Bultmann has done justice to Israel's reaction against the mythical world view, with its cyclical understanding of time. Even apocalyptic, which draws most heavily upon mythological imagery, has broken with the pagan view of "the eternal return." The *Endzeit* which it portrays is not a repetition of the *Urzeit* but rather its crown and fulfillment. Apocalyptic writers view history as a purposive drama which moves with the certainty of a well-devised plan toward the conclusion which God had in view from the beginning. Admittedly, "the old mythological themes rise to a new crescendo" in the apocalyptic movement, as Frank Cross observes, but this new formulation of the faith of Israel "is still firmly controlled by a historical framework."

> The primordial events of creation and the eschatological events of the new creation are typologically related, but are held apart by the events of human history so that unlike the movement of myth, the primordial event and the eschatological event never merge in a cultic "Now." [35]

Bultmann has drawn attention, however, to a significant point: apocalyptic, unlike prophecy, does not stress Israel's *Heilsgeschichte*. In Daniel, for instance, there is no typology of the old Exodus and the new, no reinterpretation *(Vergegenwärtigung)* of the sacred history of God's dealings with his people, Israel. Apocalyptic writers viewed history in *universal* terms—as a historical and even a cosmic drama which moves

---

34 On this mooted question, see especially Eichrodt, "Is Typological Exegesis an Appropriate Method?" [40] The major exponent of typology is von Rad; see his *Old Testament Theology* [126], Vol. II, especially the discussion of "The Actualization of the Old Testament in the New," pp. 319–35.

35 Frank M. Cross, "The Divine Warrior" [35], p. 18.

from the absolute beginning of time (creation) to the absolute end, when history will be completely transfigured and transformed in the New Creation (the New Heaven and the New Earth). The result of this universal view of history is that in apocalyptic the chaos myth is not historicized to refer to saving events of Israel's history (as in Second Isaiah); rather, chaos imagery is used to portray the cosmic rebellion, the demonic struggle which characterizes the whole historical drama from beginning to end. As God put down the powers of chaos at the beginning, so he will conquer the powers opposed to his reign at the end.

VI

The transition from prophecy to apocalyptic was marked by the attempt to understand at a deeper level the nature of the historical conflict in which Israel was inescapably involved owing to her location in the strategic corridor connecting the two great centers of world power: Mesopotamia to the north, and Egypt to the south. The Israelite cult, in which this struggle was portrayed as a conflict between creation and chaos, had already prepared the way for a deeper understanding of the historical struggle. Herbert May, in his important study of chaos imagery in the Old Testament, observes that this language carries a hint of "cosmic dualism."

> The enemies are manifestations of the intransigent elements which had to be quelled by Yahweh before creation could begin, and which must ever be defeated by him as he continues his activity in history. The enemy defeated by Yahweh is something more than just the enemy of Israel or of an individual Israelite; he is the enemy of Yahweh and identified with the corporate whole of Yahweh's antagonists.

He suggests, therefore, that the deeper dimension of Yahweh's victory over Israel's enemies, whether experienced as an event of the past (the Reed Sea), the present, or the future (the opening of the New Age), is "a victory over cosmic evil and wickedness, over the demonic or more properly the dragonic." [36] In other words, the awareness was dawning that the conflict of history is not a mere wrestling "with flesh and blood," but a contention against "principalities and powers" (Eph. 6:12).

This understanding was deepened and articulated by Israel's immense suffering occasioned by the fall of the nation in 587 B.C. About this time, the time of the Exile, prophets became poignantly aware that the evil of history cannot be attributed simply to man's will to disobey God, to the fact that "every imagination of the thought of his [man's] heart was only evil continually"—as the Yahwist explained historical tragedy (Gen. 6:5). Jeremiah's poetic description of returning chaos (see above, pp. 12 f.), written in the shadow of the destruction of Jerusalem and the breakup of the nation, reflects an awareness of a dimension of evil in history which cannot be explained on the basis of the covenant. The powers of chaos lurk at the depth of God's creation, restlessly striving to break beyond their bounds and engulf man's world. And this is no mere cosmological picture. In his sensitive moments man knows that his life is disturbed not only by the anxiety of guilt but also by the anxiety of meaninglessness. God's creation is threatened not only by sin but also by chaos.

One illustration of this attempt to grapple with the problem of history's evil in depth is found in apocalyptic passages where the old motif of "the foe from the North" is reinterpreted. In the early prophecies of Jeremiah this foe, though not necessarily identified with the Scythians, was thought of as coming on the stage of history. But the tragic experience of the fall of the nation and the exile of the people occasioned a transformation of this motif: increasingly the foe took on "a transhistorical, apocalyptic coloring." This change in the nature of the enemy, according to a study by Brevard Childs, is discernible in the description of the battle with Gog "in the latter years" (Ezek. 38–39):

---

36 May [100], pp. 11 f. As we shall see in the next chapter, this hint of cosmic dualism was never developed into a thoroughgoing dualism. In the biblical context it was regarded as essentially a "creaturely" conflict, not a conflict rooted in divine reality itself.

The description which began on the nebulous fringes of history has been elevated into the trans-historical, into an arena beyond direct relation to contemporary reality. Gog has become the representative of the cosmic powers of the returned chaos which Yahweh destroys in the latter days, powers which cannot be described as historical, although presented partly in historical dress.[37]

The portrayal of the powers of chaos "partly in historical dress" is apparently found in the vision in Daniel 7. According to the vision, the seer beheld the four winds of heaven stirring up "the great sea" and from this tempestuous deep came four beasts (or kingdoms), each more terrible than its predecessor (Dan. 7:1–12). Many scholars have followed Gunkel's interpretation that here we have a reference to the cosmic Sea, the chaotic Deep *(tehom)*. It is true that these beasts are not described as waging conflict with God, as in the old myths of Leviathan or Sea *(Yam)*. In using this imagery, the writer wants to symbolize *historical* powers, that is, kings and empires which oppressed the Jewish people. The brutality of these empires is brought out in the contrast between their bestial character and the human aspect of the figure who comes with the clouds of heaven (Dan. 7:13–14). Nevertheless, the origin of these beasts out of the sea, the locus of the chaotic, undoubtedly signifies that the historical evil manifest in the empires is rooted in a radical opposition to God's purpose which couches deep in his creation.

The trans-historical dimension of evil was emphasized more and more in the apocalyptic literature which flourished in the period between 200 B.C. and A.D. 100, roughly speaking. In contrast to prophecy, apocalyptic eschatology maintained a tenuous connection with the historical process. It conceived of world history as being involved in a vast cosmic drama in which the powers of evil are heading toward the final showdown with God, the creator and redeemer. To be sure, as in the apocalypse of Daniel this great drama was cryptically related to the contemporary scene. The Psalms of Solomon, which come from the middle of the first century B.C., contain

---

37 Childs, "The Enemy from the North and the Chaos Tradition" [28], p. 196.

a veiled reference to the Roman general Pompey in the expression *the pride of the dragon* (Ps. Sol. 2:29); and the Zadokite Document, fragments of which were found at Qumran, describes the "kings of the nations" as "serpents" (VIII:10).[38] But these historical allusions only indicate that the struggle waged on earth is part of a larger conflict whose scale is as vast as the cosmos.

In portraying this cosmic conflict, apocalyptic writers gave free reign to the poetic imagination. They drew deeply upon a reservoir of mythical symbolism whose ultimate sources were Babylon, Canaan, Egypt, and Persia. In the Testament of Asher, for instance, which belongs to the work known as *The Testament of the Twelve Patriarchs* (the nucleus of which probably goes back to the first century B.C.), it is said that in the last day, when the Most High comes to save not only Israel but also the Gentiles, he will "break the head of the dragon in the water" (Test. Ash. 7:3). This statement is reminiscent of Psalm 74:13 ("thou didst break the heads of the dragons on the waters") and Ugaritic parallels which we have considered. Even more striking usage of mythical symbolism appears in three different books which apparently draw upon a common tradition going back to the Babylonian creation myth. In the part of the book of Enoch known as the "Similitudes of Enoch," based on a tradition reaching back into the first century B.C., we find a passage which recalls the Babylonian myth concerning the male and female monsters Apsu and Tiamat:

> And on that day were two monsters parted, a female monster named Leviathan, to dwell in the abysses of the ocean over the fountains of the waters. But the male is named Behemoth, who occupied with his breast a waste wilderness. . . . And I besought the other angel that he should show me the might of those monsters, how they were parted on one day and cast, the one into the abysses of the sea, and the other unto the dry land of the wilderness.
>
> —I ENOCH 60:7–9

---

38 These and some of the following texts are discussed briefly by D. S. Russell, *The Method and Message of Jewish Apocalyptic* [138], pp. 122–25. The texts are found in R. H. Charles, *Apocrypha and Pseudepigrapha* [4].

If the expression *on that day* refers primarily to the time of creation, when the waters were separated from the waters (cf. Gen. 1:6), it also refers in the present context to the final judgment, when the two monsters will be subdued in accordance with the greatness of God (cf. I Enoch 60:24).[39] These same two monsters are also mentioned in the Apocalypse of Ezra (known as II Esdras or as IV Esdras in the appendix to the Vulgate), a work which comes from the latter part of the first century A.D. There it is said that these two monsters, which presumably were both sea monsters in the beginning, were separated—Leviathan being assigned to the water and Behemoth to the dry land (II Esd. 6:49–52). A slightly later apocalyptic writing called II Baruch, otherwise known as the Syriac Apocalypse of Baruch, transposed this mythical motif into an eschatological context by announcing that in the day of the Messiah the two chaos monsters will be food for the great "messianic banquet."

> And it shall come to pass when all is accomplished that was to come to pass in those parts, that the Messiah shall then begin to be revealed. And Behemoth shall be revealed from his place and Leviathan shall ascend from the sea, those two great monsters which I created on the fifth day of creation,[40] and shall have kept until that time; and then they shall be for food for all that are left.
> —II BARUCH 29:3–4

Indeed, the apocalyptic drama set forth in this writing develops the theme of kingship won in conflict with the waters of chaos, as known in ancient Babylon or Canaan.[41] Thus the appearance of the Messiah as king (II Bar. 39:7) will be followed by his defeat of the last tyrannical leader (40:1). And before the final consummation, marked by the Messiah's judgment on all peoples (73:1 ff.), the messianic banquet on the flesh of the two chaos monsters (29:3–4), and the inauguration of the

---

[39] Wisdom writers were also interested in the mysteries of the creation. Behemoth, "the first of the works of God," is described in Job 40:15–24; and Leviathan in Job 41:1–34.

[40] See Gen. 1:21: "So God created the great sea monsters [*tanninim*] . . ."; cf. Jubilees 2:11.

[41] Cf. Gray, *The Legacy of Canaan* [66], pp. 34–36.

New Age (73:1 ff.), the earth will be menaced by a flood of black waters (Chaps. 53 ff., especially 69 and 70). Interestingly, in the vision the waters rain down from a cloud which rises from "a very great sea" (53:1). The intention of the apocalypse in portraying this picture of cosmic confusion is to affirm that ultimately the Messiah will overcome the powers of chaos which now threaten the creation.

In view of the recrudescence of mythical imagery in apocalyptic literature, it is not surprising that the "sea" is regarded as the locus of insurgent powers, as in Daniel 7 where the beasts arise from the sea or in the comparable account in II (IV) Esdras (Chaps. 11 and 12) where the eagle (symbolizing the Roman Empire) also comes up from the sea (cf. Rev. 13:1). The Testament of Levi, for instance, associates the coming Day of Judgment with the breaking of the rocks, the extinguishing of the sun, and the drying of the waters (4:1). Similarly in the Assumption of Moses it is said that

> the sea shall retire into the abyss,
> and the fountains of waters shall fail,
> and the rivers shall dry up.
> —ASSUMPTION OF MOSES 10:6

According to the Sibylline Oracles: "In the last time the sea shall be dry" (V. 447) and "the deep sea and Babylon itself" will be burned up (V. 159).

In the New Testament the Apocalypse of John draws freely upon this mythical imagery, as Gunkel demonstrated in his *Creation and Chaos*. The seven-headed monster known in ancient Semitic mythology reappears (Rev. 12:3) and is explicitly identified with Satan: "the great dragon . . . that ancient serpent" (12:9). A new version of the beast rising out of the sea is presented (Chap. 13). And the apocalypse reaches its climax in the vision of "a new heaven and a new earth" in which there is no more sea.

> Then I saw a new heaven and a new earth; for the first heaven and the first earth had passed away, and the sea was no more.
> —REVELATION 21:1

Thus in apocalyptic the whole historical drama, from creation to consummation is viewed as a cosmic conflict between the divine and the demonic, creation and chaos, the kingdom of God and the kingdom of Satan. According to this view, the outcome of the conflict will be God's victorious annihilation of the powers which threaten his creation, including death which apocalyptic writers regarded as an enemy hostile to God (Isa. 25:8; Test. Levi xviii; II Esd. viii:53). Seen in this perspective, the role of the Anointed One, the Messiah, would be not just to liberate men from the bondage of sin but to battle triumphantly against the formidable powers of chaos.[42]

---

[42] For a discussion of creation mythology in rabbinical literature, see Ernst W. Ehrlich, *Die Kultsymbolik im Alten Testament und im nachbiblischen Judentum* [172], pp. 12–17.

CHAPTER
5

Creation and Conflict

THE THEME OF THIS CHAPTER was stated in its sharpest form in a book by Edwin Lewis, who for many years taught systematic theology at the Theological School of Drew University. The book appeared in the year 1948, in the wake of a catastrophic world war which had shaken the foundations of civilization. In the preface Lewis harks back to the year 1939, almost a decade earlier, when he wrote an article for a famous series in *The Christian Century* on the subject "How My Mind Has Changed in This Decade." He recalls that at that time he had given up the attempt to fit the Christian faith into the Procrustean bed of "philosophical monistic idealism" and, under the influence of a deeper appreciation of the Scriptures, had come to accept and emphasize as never before divine revelation. His determination was to expound the gospel "as it is," to elaborate its glorious and overwhelming message "especially as concerns the personal cost to God of redeeming from the blight of sin the world which of his own sovereign will he had created." In this book he tells us, however, that the more he reflected upon the concept of God's "sovereign will" the more he felt that he was still under the influence of the "monistic" point of view of his earlier years, that is, the view which traces the complexities and contradictions of historical existence to a single source or a common ground, variously called "the Absolute," "Being," or perhaps even "the will of God." The testimony of the Scriptures, he insisted, is entirely different: namely, "that the God of holy love has an Adversary with whose opposition he must continually reckon." Hence the title of his book: *The Creator and the Adversary*.[1]

What interests the reader particularly is Lewis' contention that the conflict to which the Bible bears witness is no mere historical conflict, no mere wrestling with flesh and blood. Rather, he says, "this opposition is in very much more than the will of man. It goes down to the very roots of existence." [2] Therefore Lewis presses back beyond the tumult and shouting of history to creation itself, and thus to the very first words of the Bible: "In the beginning—God." Though Lewis shies away from exegesis of the first chapter of Genesis, he ventures to say that to take this ancient declaration for granted does not require taking for granted "that in the beginning was God and nothing else." He offers this theological paraphrase:

> God never began to be. The Adversary never began to be. The "makings" of their battlefield never began to be. The only thing that began to be was the conflict itself, at least, the conflict in the form which makes creation as we know it. Creation is the issue of God's challenge to the Adversary and of the Adversary's acceptance of the challenge.[3]

Although Lewis does not use the imagery of chaos, he comes very close to it when he describes "the discreative demonic" as "the purely irrational, the purely immoral, the purely malign, the purely destructive." [4]

I

These theological statements should be read not only within the context of the Scriptures, where they must be tested ex-

---

1 Edwin Lewis, *The Creator and the Adversary* [97], pp. 7–8.

2 *Ibid.*, p. 8.

3 *Ibid.*, p. 140.

4 *Ibid.*, p. 145.

egetically, but also in the context of our times, where their meaning is clear. A generation that witnessed the unimaginably horrible crime of the liquidation of six million Jews and the nuclear annihilation of Nagasaki and Hiroshima was forced to come to terms with evil as "an alien power," as Lewis described it. That grotesque carving of the Devil in the form of a chimera that looks out broodingly from one of the towers of Notre Dame across the city of Paris has become more than a quaint adornment. The vision of evil has become all too real to our generation. It is not accidental that there has been a new interest in Dostoyevsky's dramas of evil; or that an artist like Rouault portrays the dominance of Satan in his Crucifix-ion-centered painting; or that the poet Yeats speaks in apoc-alyptic tones to our time about the return of the Anti-Christ in the form of the Beast to be born in a new nativity at Beth-lehem:

> Surely some revelation is at hand;
> Surely the Second Coming is at hand.
> The Second Coming! Hardly are those words out
> When a vast image out of Spiritus Mundi
> Troubles my sight: somewhere in sands of the desert
> A shape with lion body and the head of a man,
> A gaze blank and pitiless as the sun,
> Is moving its slow thighs, while all about it
> Reel shadows of the indignant desert birds.
> The darkness drops again; but now I know
> That twenty centuries of stony sleep
> Were vexed to nightmare by a rocking cradle,
> And what rough beast, its hour come round at last,
> Slouches toward Bethlehem to be born? [5]

To be sure, belief in a literal Devil, so objectively real that Martin Luther supposedly threw his inkpot at him in a moment of rage, has faded away under the influence of modern

---

[5] Quoted and discussed by Amos N. Wilder, *Modern Poetry and the Christian Tradition* [160], pp. 312 f. From "The Second Coming." Reprinted with permission of The Macmillan Company from *Collected Poems* (2nd ed., p. 185) by William Butler Yeats. Copyright 1924 by The Macmillan Company. Renewed 1952 by Bertha Georgie Yeats.

rationalism and secularism.[6] Nevertheless, it is significant that our time has seen the appearance of impressive commentaries on the meaning of the myth of Satan, such as C. S. Lewis' *The Screwtape Letters* or the Swiss journalist Denis de Rougement's *The Devil's Share*.[7]

Returning for a final moment to Edwin Lewis' intriguing book, there is a great deal of truth in his contention that "for the purposes of Christian interpretation, the concept of the demonic is as indispensable as the concept of the divine." [8] It can hardly be doubted that the Christian interpretation of human existence, as rooted in the Scriptures, is a *theology of conflict,* a conflict which will be resolved finally in the coming of God's kingdom, of which the victorious life, death, and resurrection of Jesus Christ are the foretaste, promise, and beginning. Yet what is the nature of this conflict to which the Scriptures bear witness? Is it rooted fundamentally in the human will? If so, it is a historical conflict, since history is the sphere of human existence. Or is the opposition to God located outside of man? If this is the case, creation is the first victorious round in the struggle between the Creator and the Adversary which is intrinsic to the very nature of reality. For each of these possibilities, according to the phenomenological analysis of Paul Ricoeur, there is a corresponding major mythical type: in the former case, the "Adamic myth," which locates evil in the human will, and in the latter the "theogonic myth" of chaos, which locates the source of the struggle within the divine itself. According to the myth of Adam ("the Fall"), evil is "posterior" to creation; it marks the beginning of a sinful history which God enters with the intention of overcoming man's recalcitrant will and reconciling the world unto himself —that is, a history of salvation *(Heilsgeschichte).* According to

---

6 For discussions of the idea of Satan in western culture, see Paul Carus, *History of the Devil* [26]; Edward Langton, *Satan, A Portrait* [95]; also S. G. F. Brandon, "The Devil in Faith and History" [21].

7 C. S. Lewis, *The Screwtape Letters* (New York: Macmillan, 1943); Denis de Rougement, *The Devil's Share* (New York: Pantheon Books, 1944).

8 E. Lewis [97], p. 133.

the other myth, "evil is coextensive with the origin of things, as primeval chaos and theogonic strife"; and since the purpose of creation was to eliminate the evil powers, "there is no history of salvation distinct from the drama of creation." [9]

From the standpoint of the New Testament, the best way to deal with this problem is to consider the myth of Satan.

II

About the time of the Second World War a great storm of controversy broke out over the proposal, advanced by Rudolf Bultmann, that the New Testament be "demythologized," that is, freed from its objective three-storied picture of the universe and understood according to its kerygmatic intention.[10] Today one cannot speak of the "myth of Satan" without due recognition of the tremendous value of this theological debate. There is surely a sense in which the scientific revolution has profoundly altered the world in which we live. Postscientific man does not live in a world swarming with evil spirits which bring about sickness, mental disorders, or mistaken choices, and we can rejoice that the acts of fanaticism prompted by the older beliefs are things of the past. One shudders to recall the terrible chapters in our own American history that deal with witchcraft and its suppression or with demoniac possession and its exorcism. There is a sense in which we *do not* and *can not* live in the world of the New Testament, where the demons had sway over men's actions and their bodies. But, paradoxically, the secularization which has emancipated us from the

---

[9] Paul Ricoeur, *The Symbolism of Evil* [132], Pt. II, Chaps. I and III.

[10] This much discussed essay appears under the title "New Testament and Mythology" [23]. Will Herberg has drawn my attention to a passage in W. F. Albright's Whidden Lectures (*New Horizons in Biblical Research* [New York: Oxford, 1966], pp. 32–33) in which he challenges the notion that New Testament Christianity presupposes a three-storied view of the universe. "It is just as incongruous," Albright writes, "to say that the New Testament (or rabbinic literature, or the Old Testament is mythological because God and heaven are depicted as being 'up,' as it is to say that a person [today] believes in a geocentric universe because he speaks of the sun rising in the east and setting in the west . . ."

world of evil spirits has also ushered us into a frightening period of history when the power of evil has to be taken more
seriously than ever before. Therefore we are in a position to
understand what the myth of Satan *intends* to say about the
human situation and about God's relation to history, that is,
to grasp the meaning of the myth.

One thing should be clear to any serious student of the New
Testament: the idea of Satan cannot be dismissed as "a haphazard, occasional intrusion into the main stream of biblical
ideas." [11] Valiant attempts have been made to show that the
belief in demons is purely a situation-conditioned belief, an
evidence that early Christians were after all children of their
time, and that therefore the belief makes no greater claim upon
Christian theology than, say, the practice of footwashing. But
this attempt has failed. Here we are dealing with a belief that
belongs to the very substance of the New Testament; accordingly, the statement of Emil Brunner shows theological hon-
esty: "In the New Testament this dark background—the existence of the powers of darkness (however this may be conceived)—is integral to the story of Jesus Christ." [12]

Here it would be profitable to pause for a consideration of
the various aspects of New Testament demonology and the
way this subject is handled by each New Testament writer.
However, since our primary concern is to understand the nature of the opposition to God, a summarizing statement must
suffice. Even a superficial glance at the New Testament is
enough to disclose that the New Testament idea of Satan is far
different from the kind of demonology found among primitive
societies where people believed themselves to be surrounded by
innumerable spirits whose capricious incursions accounted for
anything which deviated from the normal course of things.

---

[11] Of the various studies which treat the significance of Satan in New
Testament writings, see especially the monograph by Trevor Ling, *The
Significance of Satan* [99]; see also Paul S. Minear, *Eyes of Faith* [107], pp.
101–11.

[12] Quoted by T. Ling [99] from Emil Brunner, *The Christian Doctrine
of Creation and Redemption*, trans. Olive Wyon (London: Lutterworth,
1952), p. 134.

Perhaps the major characteristic of New Testament demonology is the view that the demons are agents or manifestations of the *Evil One,* who is the head of a kingdom of evil.[13] Evil is portrayed not as a plurality of haphazard forces but rather as an empire ruled by a single Power which, according to the terms of the myth, is personified as Satan. And over against the kingdom of evil, in fundamental and irreconcilable opposition to it, stands the kingdom of God. The Messiah, as portrayed in the Gospels, is the aggressor against Satan. By word and deed he precipitates the conflict and gives evidence of the final victory of God's kingdom, which is even now at hand. The conflict is exemplified in the famous Beelzebul controversy in which the accusation was made against Jesus: "He is possessed by Beelzebul, and by the prince of demons he casts out the demons." The incident is found in both Markan (Mark 3:22–27) and Q (Matt. 12:22–30; 9:32–34; Luke 11:14–15, 17–23) versions.

> And he [Jesus] called them to him, and said to them in parables, "How can Satan cast out Satan? If a kingdom is divided against itself, that kingdom cannot stand. And if a house is divided against itself, that house will not be able to stand. And if Satan has risen up against himself and is divided, he cannot stand, but is coming to an end. But no one can enter a strong man's house and plunder his goods, unless he first binds the strong man; then indeed he may plunder his house.
>
> —MARK 3:23–27

Considering the pervasiveness of the theme of conflict with Satan in the New Testament, it is somewhat surprising that demonology lies out on the periphery of the Old Testament.[14] The comparative dearth of Old Testament references to demonology is all the more striking in view of the great importance of the subject in the religions of other peoples of antiquity.

---

[13] See Paul Minear's discussion of "Satan's Kingdom" [107], pp. 104–8.

[14] According to P. Minear ([107], pp. 94–101), the form of opposition to God in the Old Testament is idolatry. "The role which the idol plays in the Old Testament," he observes, "is taken in the New Testament by Satan" (p. 101). This thesis throws light on something evident within the Old Testament itself, namely, the degradation of the gods of the nations to demons (e.g. Deut. 32:17).

Doubtless if we had more immediate access to the religion of Israel as practiced by the general run of the people we would discover that demonology had a greater place than in the present texts of the Old Testament, which have been severely edited on the basis of the Yahweh faith. In the early period Israelites must have shared with other peoples the belief in *daimonia,* or anonymous divine powers, capable of either good or evil influence, that were active alongside the major deities.[15] Thus we read here and there about *shedim* (Deut. 32:17; Ps. 106:37), a term which in Akkadian could refer to either a beneficial or a harmful demon; or we hear of *she'irim* ("hairy ones"), apparently some kind of hairy, goatlike demons that inhabited desert places (Lev. 17:7; II Chron. 11:15; the RSV translates "satyrs" in Isa. 13:21; 34:14). Now and then there are references to specific demons, such as Azazel, apparently a demon inhabiting the wilderness (Lev. 16:8) or Lilith, another demon haunting desolate places (the RSV translates "night hag"; Isa. 34:14). But these instances are rather few and far between, and hardly provide the basis for an Israelite demonology. As T. H. Gaster observes, "demons often survive as figures of speech (e.g. 'gremlins') long after they have ceased to be figures of belief," and this may account for a number of the occurrences in the Old Testament.[16]

Israel's faith stressed the sovereignty of Yahweh's will to such an uncompromising extent that it refused to allow the control to slip into the hand of some rival power, whether a good demon or an evil demon. Men believed that Yahweh was the sole source of good and evil, of light and darkness, of life and death. In the Exodus story, for instance, Moses' complaint that he was slow of speech evoked the divine rebuke: "Who has made man's mouth? Who makes him dumb, or deaf, or seeing, or blind? Is it not I, Yahweh?" (Ex. 4:11). Or in the "Song of Moses" (Deut. 32), an early "Covenant Lawsuit," Israel is re-

---

15 See the illuminating article by T. H. Gaster, "Demon, Demonology" [59]. He points out that the Hebrew equivalent of "demon" in its original sense of Greek *daimon* (think of Socrates following his *daimon!*) is simply *'el* or *'elohim,* words usually translated "god."

16 *Ibid.,* p. 818.

buked for the fact that the people "were unmindful of the Rock that begot you, and you forgot the God who gave you birth"—forgetfulness demonstrated by sacrifice to *shedim* ("demons"), that is, the Canaanite gods who were actually no-gods (Deut. 32:15–18). According to this poet, Israel has failed to realize that Yahweh alone is the source of both what is harmful and what is beneficial:

> "See now that I, even I, am he,
>   and there is no god beside me;
> I kill and I make alive;
>   I wound and I heal;
>   and there is none that can deliver out of my hand."
>
> —DEUTERONOMY 32:39

This ancient insistence that Yahweh alone is the source of good and evil was reiterated with theological profundity in the prophecy of Second Isaiah, perhaps in oblique criticism of Iranian (Zoroastrian) dualism, which regarded the world as a battleground between Ahura-Mazda, the supreme god of light and goodness, and the evil Angra Mainyu with his legions of demons *(Daevas)*.[17]

> I am Yahweh, and there is no other,
>   besides me there is no God;
>   I gird you, though you do not know me,
> that men may know, from the rising of the sun
>   and from the west, that there is none besides me;
>   I am Yahweh, and there is no other.
> I form light and create darkness,
>   I make weal and create woe,
>   I am Yahweh, who do all these things.
>
> —ISAIAH 45:5–7

As we well know, such sublime affirmations of God's sovereignty are difficult to maintain theologically or philosoph-

---

[17] Gaster maintains ([59], p. 821) that in the post-exilic and intertestamental periods, under the influence of Iranian ideas, the daimons were turned into devils, that is, they were transformed "from anonymous gods into distinctive forces of evil, whose function was not only to inflict misfortune and disaster but also deliberately to seduce mankind from an ordered and profitable mode of life."

ically in the face of the hard reality of evil. An interesting biblical illustration of the problem is found in the story of David's attempt to extend his power into areas formerly controlled by the tribes by "numbering" all of Israel. The story as told in II Samuel 24 reflects the conviction that David's grasp for greater power was an infringement upon Yahweh's sovereignty, that is, an act of *hybris* which brought upon itself, like an inexorable chain-reaction, divine judgment in the form of a plague. According to this way of thinking, the natural calamity came not by some evil demon but by the power of Yahweh, and so the chapter begins: "Again the anger of Yahweh was kindled against Israel, and he incited David against them, saying, 'Go, number Israel and Judah' " (II Sam. 24:1). But about five centuries later, when the Chronicler wanted to use this story because its climax dealt with the acquisition of the site of the temple, theological sensitivity had become sharper, and therefore he made a significant change: "*Satan* stood up against Israel, and incited David to number Israel" (I Chron. 21:1). This is one of three passages in the Old Testament, all of them from the post-exilic period, in which the figure of Satan is mentioned. The earliest of these is found in the prologue to the book of Job (Chaps. 1 and 2) where *the Satan* (with the definite article!) is singled out as a member of Yahweh's heavenly council. His function as Yahweh's attendant is to act as a prosecutor (cf. our expression "the Devil's Advocate"); in this original sense *the* Satan is "the Adversary," the one who puts men to the test. Likewise in one of Zechariah's visions *the* Satan is a member of the heavenly court whose job is to accuse men of wrong (Zech. 3:1–2). In none of these passages, however, is *the Satan* the archfiend and ringleader of rebellious forces opposed to God's rule, though admittedly the passage in I Chronicles (where *Satan* is used as a personal name, without the definite article) is a clear anticipation of developments which took place in late biblical Judaism and in Christianity. It is worthy of note that in the prologue to the book of Job, where *the Satan* is a member in good standing of Yahweh's heavenly court, the Adversary is only the *immediate* agent of

suffering (Job 2:7), for both the permission and the power to
afflict Job had been delegated to him by Yahweh.

The fact is that before the immensities of suffering forced
Israel to grapple more profoundly with historical evil in wisdom writings and apocalyptic literature, prophets, priests, and
teachers were able to account sufficiently for the woes of life
in terms of the doctrine of sin. The main opposition with
which Yahweh had to deal, according to the classical prophets,
was the recalcitrance of Israel's will; therefore the sufferings
of the people at the hands of the Assyrians and Babylonians
were interpreted as Yahweh's discipline. In other words, the
opposition to God's purpose was understood to be fundamentally a historical conflict, rooted in the human will, whether
that recalcitrance manifested itself in the hardheartedness of
Pharaoh, the stubborn infidelity of Israel, or the pretensions
of a world ruler who refused to accept his place as the "rod"
of Yahweh's purpose (Isa. 10:5–16). Admittedly, to Israelite interpreters God's creation also seemed to be menaced by forces
lurking at the edge of history ("the sea," "darkness"), though
this mythical chaos imagery, in accordance with the historical
interests of Israel's faith, was generally historicized to show
Yahweh's sovereignty over historical opposition (see above, pp.
132–37). In Israel's understanding the major menace to creation
lay in the contingency of human freedom, not in trans-human,
trans-historical powers of chaos. Edmund Jacob, after discussing Old Testament testimonies to "the residues of chaos which
existed before creation," rightly puts the accent on man's culpability.

> The sin which comes from man is a still graver threat weighing
> down upon the creation; created to be king of creation, man, by
> his disobedience to the divine command, has drawn into his fall
> this creation which was entrusted to him.[18]

---

[18] Edmund Jacob, *Theology of the Old Testament* [81], pp. 140–41. It
is not clear, however, how much weight Jacob gives to the "residues of
chaos" when he says (p. 140) that "in spite of its perfection creation is un-
ceasingly menaced by two forces [darkness, sea] which have not been created by Yahweh but have simply been subjected to him."

III

The objection may be raised that a major exception to this emphasis upon man's culpability in the preexilic period was the great work of the Yahwist which begins with a portrayal of "the fall of man" under the cunning influence of the serpent. At first glance, it is tempting to suppose that here the serpent signifies a power of evil external to man, namely "that ancient serpent, who is called the Devil and Satan, the deceiver of the whole world," as we read in the Christian Apocalypse (Rev. 12:9).

Careful study will disclose, however, that in the Yahwist's narrative the serpent does not have the mythical significance evident in other passages. This is not the serpent of chaos that lurks at the bottom of the sea, to which Amos alluded (9:3). It is not "Leviathan the fleeing serpent, Leviathan the twisting serpent" (Isa. 27:1) which the Little Apocalypse of Isaiah appropriated from the Ugaritic myth of the smiting of Lotan (see above, pp. 134 f.). It is not even the serpent with healing powers that Moses lifted up in the wilderness and which continued to be an object of veneration until the time of Hezekiah's reform (Num. 21:4–9; II Kings 18:4). Rather, the Yahwist narrator says explicitly that the serpent was merely one of the wild creatures that Yahweh had made, a creature distinguished from others by his cunning (Gen. 3:1).

To be sure, if one could trace the history of tradition back beyond the Yahwist's story he might reach a stage in which the serpent was a chthonic deity, a god of earth, who was hostile to the celestial deities. Even in the present form of the story there is something strange about the serpent: its uncanny wisdom, its ability to talk (and talk theologically!), its (implied) original erect posture, its apparent enmity toward God, its heavy penalty of curse. There are other traces, too, of pre-Yahwistic tradition, such as the deity's fear that man might attain equality with him (Gen. 3:22) or the unexplained presence of the tree of life (2:9; 3:22), a frequent motif in ancient art and literature. Yet whatever the tradition was formerly, it has been profoundly modified by Israel's retelling. In the process of recasting the old tradition, the Yahwist has "de-divinized" the serpent, so that it is just a snake.[19] The story as it has come down to us is not concerned with the origin of the serpent's cunning, the reason for its apparent insolence toward the deity, or the imposition of a test upon the man and woman; and hence the serpent motif is a long way off from the Satan of the postexilic period, the archenemy of God who foments a rebellion that spreads through the whole creation.

In the Yahwist's story the emphasis falls upon the freedom of man. Unlike the animals, who respond instinctively to their environment, man has the capacity to imagine and to reach out for a possibility and thus to transcend his limitation. This freedom, which enables man to "make history," the narrator expresses by drawing a picture of a concrete situation, using traditional imagery. In accordance with the ancient view that the serpent is characterized by wisdom (see the New Testament injunction to "be wise as serpents and innocent as doves," Matt. 10:16), he stresses the wisdom or subtlety of mind that senses the intriguing possibilities in man's concrete situation— possibilities which fascinate, lure, and tempt man to reach beyond himself, even to be "like God" (Gen. 3:5). If it is necessary to convert the concrete picture into an abstract statement, it may be said that the serpent "would be a part of ourselves which we do not recognize; he would be the seduction of ourselves by ourselves, projected into the seductive object" [20] though this interpretation is a bit too "psychological" or "sub-

---

[19] Flemming Hividberg, in an article on "The Canaanitic Background of Genesis I–III" [76], thinks that the story reflects a polemic against Prince Baal (Bel Zebul), "Yahweh's great adversary in the ancient struggle for the soul of Israel." The serpent allegedly was a Baal symbol—a male (phallic) image, which explains why the serpent tempts the woman. The Yahwist, according to this view, downgraded the serpent by saying that it has only the wisdom of cunning, not the power of life. Hence "the old Jewish-Christian belief that the serpent is the devil is far more historically true than late Judaism and early Christianity could conceive." If, however, the Yahwist intended such a polemic, why was he not explicit?

[20] P. Ricoeur [132], Pt. II, Chap. III.

jective" to do full justice to the Old Testament emphasis on the evil which presents itself to men socially, that is, in the concrete situation. Paul Ricoeur, who recognizes the validity of the anthropological interpretation of Genesis 3, seems to be puzzled unnecessarily about why pre-Yahwistic elements of tradition survive in undigested form—a phenomenon which, it should be noted, is evidenced elsewhere in the Yahwist epic (e.g. Gen. 32:22–32). He suggests that the Yahwist intentionally retained the serpent, without completely demythologizing it, in order to stress "the radical externality of evil." He observes:

> The Jews themselves, although they were well armed against demonology by their intransigent monotheism, were constrained by truth, as Aristotle would say, to concede something, to concede as much as they could without destroying the monotheistic basis of their faith, to the great dualisms which they were to discover after the exile. The theme of the serpent represents the first landmark along the road of the Satanic theme which, in the Persian epoch, permitted the inclusion of a near-dualism in the faith of Israel.[21]

If the Yahwist really retained the serpent in order to suggest the origin of evil in "a prehuman, demonic reality," as though to avoid putting the burden of guilt completely upon man, it is remarkable that no hint of this radically external evil is given elsewhere in the Yahwist epic. Indeed, the hint is so slight in Genesis 3 that Ricoeur himself, after his superb and subtle exposition of the story, concludes that "the biblical myth, in spite of Eve and the serpent, remains 'Adamic,'—that is to say, anthropological." [22]

It may well be that the great interpreters of Israel's faith, such as the Yahwist or the classical prophets, were at fault in placing so much emphasis upon Israel's sin as the root of historical troubles and thereby locating the opposition to God exclusively in the human will. But at least we should give them

---

21 *Loc. cit.* This line of argument raises the question which Will Herberg has formulated sharply: "If evil is 'radically *external*,' how can it be 'part of ourselves'?"

22 *Loc. cit.*

full credit for emphasizing the magnitude of this conflict. Trevor Ling seems to adopt too quickly the view that the prophetic analysis was fundamentally defective for "the prophets did not fully realize the nature of sin, and regarded it too exclusively as the immediate choice of the individual will." [23] This hardly does justice to the prophetic insistence that ever since the entrance into Canaan, as Hosea said, or ever since the time of the Exodus, as Ezekiel declared,[24] Israel had been caught in a history of sin—a movement of evil that had reached such momentum and proportions that the present generation seemed to be in helpless and hopeless bondage. It is quite true that prophets call upon individuals to seek good and not evil (cf. Amos 5:14–15), and Ezekiel in particular stresses the responsibility of the individual for his own sins to counteract a fatalistic view of the influence of past sins (Ezek. 18). But the prophets were aware of the corporate and historical dimension of evil. The evil which they exposed was not just the fruit of the individual will. Evil had the aspect of externality as well as individuality. In a sense, it was something outside the individual, prior to the individual; a reality that was "already there" and which the individual encountered. Evil was, in the prophetic analysis, a power transmitted socially through the generations, operative in interpersonal relations, structured in society.[25] The Adamic myth is theologically consistent with the prophetic analysis; for it only universalizes the sin operative in Israel's history by tracing this history back to the first man, who is the typical man.

As we have seen in the previous chapter, the postexilic period was the time when wisdom writers and apocalyptic seers

---

[23] Ling [99], pp. 4–5, where he refers to the position of Canon Quick.

[24] See my *Understanding the Old Testament* [11], pp. 248–50 (on Hosea) and pp. 366–67 (on Ezekiel).

[25] Walter Rauschenbusch was aware of the corporate dimension of sin when he spoke of "the power of social transmission . . . the authority of the social group in justifying, urging, and idealizing wrong, and . . . the decisive influence of economic profit in the defense and propagation of evil." (Quoted by Reinhold Niebuhr, *The Nature and Destiny of Man* [New York: Scribner, 1947], Vol. I, p. 246, from Rauschenbusch's *A Theology for the Social Gospel*.)

attempted to grapple with the problem of historical evil more radically than had been done before in Israelite tradition. However, rather than seeing this period as a time for remedying a supposed defect in prophetic understanding, it is important to recognize that the apocalyptists actually built upon and elaborated the corporate conception of evil already inherent in prophecy. The main difference was that these writers, instead of portraying evil as a reality in Israel's history and summoning the people to repentance, took the whole drama of world history into their purview, with the result that the corporate character of evil was understood to have far wider dimensions and far deeper roots than the prophets had ever realized. The externality of evil was expressed by saying that the demons seduce men to do evil, incite men to commit sin, as though the initiative—though, of course, not the *decision*—lies outside of man.

The seductive role of the demons received great stress in the years before the dawn of the Christian era, for instance in this passage from the Book of Jubilees (ca. 150 B.C.), also known as "The Little Genesis" because it is essentially a commentary on Genesis: "The unclean demons began to lead astray children of the sons of Noah, and to make to err, and to destroy them" (Jubilees 10:1).[26] But above all it was believed that evil, with imperialistic design, had extended its influence throughout the whole creation, both the celestial and terrestrial realms. The vast empire of evil was believed to be under the leadership of "the prince of demons" sometimes known as Mastemah, Belial, or Azazel, but in the Christian period as Satan or the Devil. Thus the outlook extended beyond history into the cosmos. Where formerly the tendency had been to view the cosmos in a historical perspective, now the emphasis was upon viewing history in a cosmic perspective. And in this cosmic context the theme of "creation versus chaos" becomes prominent once again.

---

26 See further D. S. Russell, *The Method and Message of Jewish Apocalyptic* [138], Chap. IX. See also E. Langton, *Essentials of Demonology* [94].

IV

In his book *Creation and Chaos,* which lies at the basis of this study, Gunkel noticed that the old theogonic myth of chaos eventually coalesced with the myth of Satan. In the metaphorical language of apocalyptic writings, Satan, the archenemy of God who will finally be overthrown at the consummation of the historical drama, was identified with the Enemy, whose power was broken but not completely destroyed at the time of creation. Here it should be recalled that the full scope of Gunkel's work was "Creation and Chaos in Beginning-time and End-time" and that he was concerned to show the correspondence between *Urzeit* and *Endzeit* in biblical eschatology.

We have already noticed (on pp. 134–43) the recrudescence of the old myth of the conflict between the Creator and the waters of chaos in apocalyptic literature. Apocalyptic writers wanted to say, in the spirit of Paul, that the conflict which men experience in history is no ordinary struggle with human powers but a struggle against "the wiles of the devil." [27]

> For we are not contending against flesh and blood, but against the principalities, against the powers, against the world rulers of this present darkness, against the spiritual hosts of wickedness in the heavenly places.
>
> —EPHESIANS 6:12

According to this view, evil does not originate in man or in history; it has, rather, a trans-human, a trans-historical source which the religious imagination indicates in the imagery of the old chaos mythology.

As we would expect, the old chaos imagery is revived especially in the Christian Apocalypse, the Revelation to John, which abandons the language of ordinary prose and portrays in highly imaginative language the eschatological horizon of the historical drama. Writing in a time when the Christian community was oppressed and persecuted by Rome, this author

---

[27] On this subject see G. B. Caird, *Principalities and Powers: A Study in Pauline Theology* [25].

adapted traditional symbolism, some of it found within the
Old Testament and some drawn from extra-biblical sources,
to the expression of the Christian hope. Just as the apocalypse
of Daniel had represented the world empires as evil beasts
emerging from the sea, so the Christian Apocalypse portrayed
the beast (Rome) as coming up from the sea (Chap. 13); and it
announced that when God's victory is complete the sea will be
no more and that there will be no more darkness (Rev. 21:1;
22:5). It is especially striking that in this writing Satan is identified with the primeval dragon, "the ancient serpent" (12:9;
20:2) and is described specifically as "a great red dragon, with
seven heads" in language which echoes ancient Canaanite mythology (cf. Ps. 74:13; and above, pp. 134 f.). First his opposition to God broke out in the heavenly sphere but he was defeated and cast down to the earth, where he "poured water
like a river out of his mouth after the woman [the Church], to
sweep her away with the flood" (12:15). In this view Satan is
none other than the monster of chaos who, according to the
pagan myth, was opposed to God from the foundation of the
world.

In the Christian Apocalypse the conflict against Satan is
waged by Christ, the agent of God. Of course, the theme of the
Messiah's conquest of the powers of chaos is also found in non-
Christian apocalyptic literature, for instance, in the Apocalypse of Baruch where the establishment of the Messiah as
king is followed by the threat of a flood of black waters upon
the earth; this in turn is the prelude to his final judgment upon
all peoples and the messianic banquet on Leviathan and Behemoth (see above, pp. 141 f.). This combination of the motif of
the messianic king and the motif of the victory over the waters
of chaos goes back, we have noticed, to the Israelite cult in the
pre-exilic period. In the great festivals when Yahweh was acclaimed as king, an important role was played by the reigning
king, who acted as mediator between God and people. "The
installation of such a prince," John Gray writes, "was itself a
manifestation and warrant of the triumph of Cosmos over
Chaos, and the king's ascendancy was the counterpart of the

Kingship of God, a conception which is expressed in the royal psalms ii and cx." Apocalyptic literature no longer presupposes this cultic *Sitz im Leben*. However, the imagery survives from the old cultic usage, though transposed into a higher key; for "the anointed agent of God came to be what he had never been before, the supernatural Messiah of apocalyptic, the agent of the absolute consummation of God's order when the present world order has been abolished." [28]

Seen against this background, we can understand why the New Testament portrays the Messiah, the Anointed of God, standing at the very storm center of the cosmic conflict between the kingdom of God and the kingdom of Satan. What Israel experienced in the cult—when the king represented the people before God in an enactment of God's triumph over the powers of chaos—was now proclaimed to be taking place outside the sphere of the cult, in the places of everyday life and in the tangled fabric of human relationships. The New Testament wants to say, *mutatis mutandis,* that the words and works of Jesus, the Messiah, were indeed "manifestations and warrants of the triumph of Cosmos over Chaos," that is, the triumph of God's kingdom over all the powers of evil and darkness.

It is true that the imagery of chaos almost disappears in the Gospels and Epistles of the New Testament and does not become prominent again until the Apocalypse of John. The theme of the conflict between Christ and Satan is prominent, however, and even the language employed to describe the conflict sometimes echoes the mythical imagery. In a recent essay Howard Kee has drawn attention to the usage of the Greek verb *epitiman,* which is often translated "rebuke" in the exorcism stories of Mark, a verb that is found in several Qumran texts in its Semitic equivalent, *ga'ar.*[29] This verb he traces back into the Old Testament where in a number of instances the texts speak of God's "rebuke" of the waters of chaos (e.g. Pss. 18:16; 104:7; 106:9). The precedent for this he finds in Ug-

---

[28] John Gray, *The Legacy of Canaan* [66], pp. 35–36.
[29] Howard C. Kee, "The Terminology of Mark's Exorcism Stories" (unpublished).

aritic literature where the same verb is used of Baal's struggle to gain the victory over the adversary known as Sea and River.[30] This language, it is alleged, when used in Mark's exorcism stories, has "the connotation of divine conflict with hostile powers, the outcome of which is the utterance of the powerful word by which the demonic forces are brought under control." For instance, right at the outset of his Gospel, Mark tells the story of the healing of a demoniac in the synagogue to show that through Jesus' exorcism the kingdom of God has drawn near (1:15). Jesus' casting out of demons is the evidence that Satan's rule is being overcome. Accordingly, the demon, recognizing the authority of Jesus, cries out: "Have you come to destroy us?" (1:24). "The demon recognizes," says Kee, "not merely that he has met his match, but the end of the whole cosmic struggle of Satan and his hosts against God is now certain to end in the defeat of the demonic powers." And when Jesus "rebukes" the demon, this is no mere reprimand; rather, it is "the word of command by which God's agent defeats his enemies, thus preparing for the coming of God's kingdom." The conclusion of this study is that the New Testament miracle stories, at least in their *earliest* stratum, do not belong in the setting of Hellenistic wonder-workers but rather in the setting of the demonology characteristic of apocalyptic Judaism.

While the New Testament shares with apocalyptic writings a view of the cosmic dimensions of evil, it is not fundamentally otherworldly in its outlook. On the contrary, the early Christian community declared in various ways that in Christ, God had begun his great renovation of the earth, his new creation. The Resurrection, as Amos Wilder reminds us, was for early Christians "the immediate prelude to the redemption of man and nature, the final overthrow of Satan. It was not an isolated event but part of God's final new creation." [31] To use the language of the myth: Satan, who, in the beginning, had chal-

---

30 Texts found in C. H. Gordon, *Ugaritic Handbook:* 68:28 and 137:24 ("Analectia Orientalia," 35; Rome, 1947).

31 Wilder, *Otherworldliness and the New Testament* [161], p. 97.

lenged and attempted to usurp God's sovereignty and who, in
the end, would be overthrown and destroyed, had already been
defeated. His power had been broken, as evidenced in the
wonders of the new age that was dawning—the exorcisms, the
healings, the forgiveness of sins, the victory over death. The
result of this great emancipation from the powers of evil was
that man was restored to the place intended for him in God's
creation—a king "crowned with glory and honor" to whom the
whole of God's domain has been given to enjoy and to manage
(see Ps. 8).

V

Finally, we must face the question of the theological implications of the myth of Satan with respect to the problem of evil,
especially as the myth came to be fused with the myth of chaos.
Does the chaos myth merely provide imagery which adds richness and depth to the presentation of a dramatic conflict which,
in the last analysis, is essentially historical, that is, rooted in
creaturely opposition to the Creator? Or does this imagery intend to locate evil not only outside of man but even before
creation, as Edwin Lewis dared to suggest in his discussion of
"the Creator and the Adversary"?

It has often been emphasized that Satan's opposition is conceived to occur *within* the overruling sovereignty of God.
Therefore the theme of the conflict between the Creator and
the Adversary does not imply an absolute dualism, such as that
found in Zoroastrianism, where Angra Mainyu, the power of
evil, is an independent power whose origin is not traceable to
the supreme god, Ahura-Mazda. This point can hardly be
denied. The myth presupposes that Satan is only a *quasi*-inde-
pendent power in history. Its portrayal of the postcreation rise
of the power of evil pictures Satan as one of the angels of
Yahweh's heavenly council who went berserk and fomented a
revolution which spread from heaven to earth. In Jewish apocalyptic circles it was believed that Genesis 6:1–4, the strange
story of the marriage of the "sons of God" and the daughters
of men, was actually an account of the fall of the heavenly

watchers or angels who gave birth to demons through their unnatural union with mortals.[32] Not only was Satan's revolution, according to the mythical portrayal, subsequent to the creation and thus a flaw arising out of God-given creaturely freedom, but in apocalyptic eschatology Satan was conceived as the leader of a history-long rebellion which in the last day will be completely quelled. Satan, therefore, is subordinate to God, and ultimately will be destroyed. His authority is limited to "the present age," when men experience both the "already" and the "not yet" of God's victory in the conflict of history. God has given him only a limited amount of rope, so to speak, and he cannot go beyond the bounds. As Paul Minear observes: "It is God who permits him to sell his wares, who limits the bounds of his dominion, who precipitates the final struggle that reveals both the present power and the final impotence of the rebel king." [33] Thus the "dualism" which the myth of Satan portrays is not a metaphysical or ontological dualism (as in Zoroastrianism, Gnosticism, Manichaeanism, etc.) but a historical dualism: a conflict which occurs between the beginning and the consummation of the historical drama.

It is significant that in the New Testament, Satan is fundamentally a parasite on man's freedom. In his study *The Significance of Satan* Trevor Ling concludes, after an examination of the New Testament data, that Satan's power is so closely dependent upon human sin that Satan has no reality apart from the exercise of human freedom. Satan is not a power that exists independently: the author of "Satanic" sin in contrast to human sin. Rather, Satan exists in the sphere of man's freedom. Ling paraphrases the myth by saying that Satan is "the spirit of unredeemed man's collective life, that which domi-

---

32 In I Enoch (Ethiopic Enoch), which includes material reaching back into the second century B.C., the origin of the evil spirits is traced to the union of the watchers of heaven with mortal women (9:8–9; 15:1–12). Through this intercourse between the heavenly and earthly spheres, men learned "all the secrets of the angels, and all the violence of the Satans, and all their powers"—such as the making of instruments for war or the use of cosmetics for seductive purposes (65:6–8; 69:4–15).

33 Minear [107], p. 106.

nates the individual and stifles his growth in truly personal life; a spirit, moreover, which is characterized by a constant effort towards self-deification." The New Testament, he insists, was talking about "the spirit of a society, a society alienated from God," and not necessarily about the Satan of medieval legend.[34]

This exposition of the meaning of the myth of Satan opens up possibilities for contemporary historical understanding. Along the same line Harvey Cox, in his much-discussed paperback, *The Secular City,* speaks of the Church's role as "cultural exorcist." Recognizing that exorcism was central in Jesus' ministry, he insists that "we must get behind the prescientific images of spirits and demons to the reality they expressed." In the New Testament, he says, these images designated "the subpersonal forces and suprapersonal influences which warped and twisted human life." And in our time these could be the economic pressures, the cultural stereotypes, the repressed and projected feelings which demand that people act in bondage to certain roles. To use Cox's example from the Civil Rights Movement, "the modern equivalent of casting out demons" would be both removing the prejudice of the white man and exorcising what Martin Luther King calls the "slave mentality" of the Negro.[35]

When the myth of Satan is considered by itself, that is, without any connection with the myth of chaos, this is a helpful reinterpretation for our time, although if one ignores the susceptibility of the individual to external influences of society, he tends to get a one-sided picture, as though the individual—a la Rousseau—were innocent and good in himself and were perverted only by social structures. It must be remembered that according to the terms of the biblical myth, the demons may "seduce" men, but the decision and therefore the responsibility lies with the individual. Nevertheless, the Satan myth does indeed expose man's involvement in evil which lies outside the individual will in the sense that evil is *there* already as a con-

34 Ling [99], pp. 83 f.
35 Harvey Cox, *The Secular City* (New York: Macmillan, 1965), Chap. 7.

ditioning factor of the society into which one is born. The "malign power of [one's] own societary life to dominate him and thus to destroy personality" is both suprapersonal and subpersonal, insofar as economic pressures, stereotyped patterns of social behavior, or chauvinistic nationalism may have this malignant influence. So interpreted, Satan is indeed a parasite upon human society, a power whose sovereignty is historically limited. But what shall we say about the dimension of reality indicated by the imagery of chaos, and especially the identification of Satan with the primordial powers of chaos?

It must be reiterated that biblical monotheism tolerates no thoroughgoing dualism which traces the origin of the historical conflict between God and evil back before man to creation, in which case evil would be coextensive with the divine. The evil with which the Bible deals primarily is the evil which came after God's creation, the evil which spoiled and corrupted the creation which came from God with his approving judgment, "very good" (Gen. 1:31). Evil is the fruit of the freedom of the creature. In that sense, it may be said to be a *historical* opposition to God's purpose, an opposition that will be finally overcome when God's creative (redemptive) work in history is complete. Even when, under the influence of Zoroastrian ideas, the dualism became most intense in apocalyptic literature, it remained a historical dualism or, better, an "eschatological dualism" in which the conflict is between "this age" and "the age to come." In the New Testament Satan's power is not over the cosmos understood as the order of nature but over the cosmos understood as the historical age *(aion)*; therefore "history remains the primary sphere within which Satan operates." [36]

It must be admitted, however, that within the Bible, despite its emphasis upon God's overruling sovereignty, there is some tension with this view, owing to the use of the myth of chaos. It is noteworthy that even the Priestly writer, who more than

---

[36] Minear [107], pp. 105, 106. See also the discussions of "cosmos, cosmology" indexed in Rudolf Bultmann, *Theology of the New Testament* [22].

any other writer in the Old Testament demythologized the old myth of chaos, did not destroy the myth completely, but allowed it to remain as a "faded myth" or a "broken myth." [37] In Israel's poetic literature, where the mythical symbolism is used more boldly, the same process of demythologization has been at work. Commenting on the presence of the chaos motif in Psalm 104 (especially vss. 5–9), Samuel Terrien observes:

> The myth of the titanic pride of the ocean has left its trace in the psalmist's poetic idiom, but its "mythical essentiality" has been broken, because the pre-existent antagonism between two deified forces of chaos and order has been transformed into *a temporally bound revolt which belongs to the realm of history*.[38]

The chaos myth, as we have seen in previous chapters, had an important place in the Jerusalem cult, where it was largely historicized; eventually it was revived in apocalyptic literature to portray the depth and range of historical evil.

Clearly, then, the Bible was not able to ignore the myth of chaos. If in the last analysis it was unable to historicize the myth completely, there is perhaps a slight biblical basis for the suggestion of Paul Ricoeur that perhaps "ethical monotheism itself must be transcended; it must be transcended insofar as it is ethical—perhaps also insofar as it is monotheism." He observes that while the naïve theogonic myth of antiquity is dead, it has been revived in "more refined ontotheologies," that is, theologies "according to which evil is an original element of being." From these perspectives the tragedy of existence cannot be traced exclusively to a fault in man's will; it has its roots also in "the pain of being, in a tragedy that is the tragedy of being itself." Hence he proposes that myths which stress man's culpability, such as the myth of the Fall (and, we may add, the related myth of Satan), may need to be supplemented with other myths in order that "the ethical God" presupposed in the Adamic myth "may continue to be a *Deus Absconditus* [a hidden God] and so that the guilty man it denounces may also

---

[37] Cf. Brevard Childs, *Myth and Reality* [27], p. 42.

[38] Samuel Terrien, "Creation, Cultus, and Faith in the Psalter" [146], p. 122. Italics mine.

appear as the victim of a mystery of iniquity which makes him deserving of Pity as well as of Wrath." [39]

Yet the writers of the Bible refuse to contemplate what Ricoeur calls the "terrible possibility" that the origin of evil is traceable to the sphere of the divine, and therefore "that evil is as old as the oldest of beings; that evil is the past of being; that it is that which was overcome by the establishment of the world; that God is the future of being." These words, which display a profound interpretation of the ontology expressed in the old chaos myth, help us to understand why there was an inevitable struggle between the faith of Israel and the pagan creation-faith, and why Israel sought to historicize the chaos imagery. There is a fundamental incompatability between this kind of ontology and the historical perspective of the Jewish and Christian faiths. Will Herberg has responded to Ricoeur's query with typical vigor and incisiveness: "If there is a 'tragedy of *being itself*,' then this 'pain,' this 'tragedy' will have to pervade the 'new age' as well; and this makes nonsense of the Jewish-Christian redemption. In the biblical view," he maintains, "the 'pain,' the 'tragedy' of being inheres *not* in 'being itself,' but in *fallen* (perverted) being." [40] In this connection it is appropriate to point out that in the consummation of God's historical purpose, according to the Apocalypse of John, God "will wipe away every tear from their eyes, and death shall be no more, neither shall there be mourning nor crying nor pain any more, for the former things have passed away" (Rev. 21:4).

Therefore the exponents of the biblical faith insist that the opposition to God is not rooted in the divine but in history, in the freedom of the creature. Since the conflict is waged *between* creation and consummation, man's salvation is not traced to a primordial victory at the creation which is re-enacted in the cult; rather, man's salvation rests upon a decisive historical event in which God has once-and-for-all eman-

---

[39] Paul Ricoeur, *The Symbolism of Evil* [132], Pt. II, Chaps. I and III.
[40] Herberg's rejoinder to Ricoeur was expressed in personal correspondence.

cipated men from the power of evil, darkness, and the chaotic
dimensions of human existence. In the faith of the Christian
church this crucial event is God's victory in Jesus Christ which,
as Paul interprets it, has historical and cosmic implications.

> Who shall separate us from the love of Christ? Shall tribulation, or
> distress, or persecution, or famine, or nakedness, or peril, or sword?
> . . . No, in all these things we are more than conquerors through
> him who loved us. For I am sure that neither death, nor life, nor
> angels, nor principalities, nor things present, nor things to come,
> nor powers, nor height, nor depth, nor anything else in all crea-
> tion, will be able to separate us from the love of God in Christ
> Jesus our Lord.
>
> —ROMANS 8:35, 37–39

Epilogue

THE LANGUAGE OF CREATION AND CHAOS sounds strange to our ears but it is not necessarily alien to our lives. Indeed, we have found ourselves on vaguely familiar territory during this exploration of the biblical understanding of existence expressed in these terms. Situated inescapably in the midst of the historical arena, we know the reality of conflict—a conflict which could explode to global or even cosmic proportions. The frightening power of evil has overwhelmed us in a dreadful apocalypse which unveils the dark depths of so-called civilized man. Moreover, we share with ancient man a poignant awareness of our involvement in the struggle between life and death which goes on in the natural world. Nature is part of our history, not just in the sense that its terrifying powers are now at our disposal but also that it acts erosively upon our lives and upon the whole edifice of human civilization. In the face of the radical contingency of existence, one sometimes feels a sense of desolation, as though the ordered and meaningful world in which we live were ever on the verge of collapse into chaos.

This study has attempted to show that although Israel borrowed the motif of "creation versus chaos" from ancient Near

Eastern religion, she reinterpreted the mythical symbolism. Creation was understood historically. Israel's testimony to the world is that man, who is tormented by the question "to be or not to be," finds who he is and what life really means not in relation to nature, with its great cycles of death and re- newal, but in relation to history, where God calls him to choose whom he will serve and summons him to participate in God's own historical purpose. Even when Israel's borrowing from the old chaos myth is heaviest, the intention in using the lan- guage is to probe the depth of history's meaning. In times of historical crisis Israel could go through the "deep waters" in the confidence that Yahweh is Lord over the Deep, over the powers of chaos. These historical experiences, not unlike our own in the perilous twentieth century, are undoubtedly re- flected in the creation story of Genesis, with its concern for the surrounding chaos. Commenting on Genesis 1:2 ("The earth was without form and void, and darkness was upon the face of the deep"), Gerhard von Rad remarks:

> This second verse speaks not only of a reality that once existed in a preprimeval period but also of a possibility that always exists. Man has always suspected that behind all creation lies the abyss of formlessness, further, that all creation is always ready to sink into the abyss of the formless, that the chaos, therefore, signifies simply the threat to everything created; and this suspicion has been a constant temptation for his faith.[1]

To the degree that we experience the threat of meaningless- ness, the fear of the void, we understand this imagery which expresses the negative side of God's creation.

Modern poetry, art, depth psychology, and philosophies of existence have helped us to recover the meaning of language which speaks about the chaotic, the demonic, the dark. In the

---

[1] Von Rad, *Genesis* [124], pp. 48 f. See also Brevard Childs, *Myth and Reality* [27], pp. 41 f., who in this connection calls attention to Karl Barth's discussion of the chaos symbolism in *Church Dogmatics* [18], III, 1, pp. 107 f.; III, 3, pp. 352 f. Dietrich Bonhoeffer, in *Creation and Fall* [19], pp. 14–18, interprets "the dark deep" as "the first sound of the power of darkness, of the Passion of Jesus Christ." The "void," he insists, is rooted in the freedom of God who creates out of nothing.

field of art, the modern spirit was foreshadowed more than a century ago by the artist Turner. An art critic points out that Turner began to break with his artistic tradition; for his art not only portrayed the aspect of "stillness and gradation of radiant light" but also the opposite aspect: "the turbulent journey through storm and catastrophe." [2] A contemporary wrote of his landscape scenes:

> They are pictures of the elements of air, earth, and water. The artist delights to go back to the first chaos of the world, or to the state of things, when the waters were separated from the dry land, and light from darkness, but as yet no living thing nor tree bearing fruit was seen on the face of the earth. All is without form and void.[3]

In the field of literature Herman Melville's classic, *Moby Dick*, a novel which draws deeply upon the chaos imagery of the Bible, foreshadowed movements in modern literature which probe beneath the surface of existence.[4] Paul Tillich, in an essay called "The Depth of Existence," observed that "the depth in religious language is often used to express the dwelling place of the evil forces, of the demonic powers, of death and hell." [5] This, of course, is a dimension of existence men would rather avoid. W. H. Auden writes:

> Heroic charity is rare;
> without it, what except despair
> can shape the hero who will dare
> the desperate catabasis
> into the snarl of the abyss

---

2 See Lawrence Gowing, *Turner: Imagination and Reality* (New York: The Museum of Modern Art; distributed by Doubleday and Co., 1966), p. 11. I am grateful to Professor Carlyle Holte of St. Olaf College for drawing my attention to this book.

3 *Ibid.*, p. 13.

4 See the discussion of "The Shaking of the Foundations" by Amos Wilder in *Modern Poetry and the Christian Tradition* [160], Chap. IX.

5 Paul Tillich, *The Shaking of the Foundations* (New York: Scribner, 1948), pp. 52-63. In his *Systematic Theology* (Chicago: University of Chicago Press, 1957), Vol. II, p. 37, he refers specifically to the struggle between divine and chaotic powers.

> that always lies just underneath
> our jolly picnic on the heath
> of the agreeable . . .[6]

But we cannot escape the katabasis into the abyss, the descent into hell, the immersion in the waters of chaos. Historical reality overwhelms us—perhaps through the event of someone's death, perhaps through historical catastrophe which shakes the foundations of the world, perhaps through some wild outbreak of nature evidenced in a destructive earthquake or a berserk man's murdering madness. And then the chaos myth speaks to us.

There is an unforgettable passage in Gladys Schmitt's novel *Confessors of the Name*. The setting is the last fateful period of the Roman Empire. The great empire, which had brought order and security to the world, was collapsing—threatened by barbarian invasions from without and weakened from within by moral corruption. At one point in the story the leading character, an intelligent, aristocratic Roman youth, recalls a terrifying dream:

> "When I was small—oh eight or nine," he said in a flat voice, "we studied the myths—our teacher told us the accepted version of the creation of the world. Chaos was there first, he said, black Chaos moving over the face of the earth, and he explained Chaos to us as best he could—reasonless confusion, blind chance, no pattern to anything, everything happening by accident in the dark, meaningless birth, meaningless death. None of the others took the thing to heart, but for some insane reason I was obsessed with it for months—I couldn't laugh, I couldn't play, I woke up in the middle of the night, screaming because I was convinced that Chaos was back again. I invented the most horrible images—maybe to torture myself—I imagined the City turned upside-down at the bottom of the sea, I imagined perpetual night with the stars raining out of the sky. . . . When I heard the rumble of a carriage at night, I would run to the window to see that it was a carriage, not the sea washing up onto the land. . . . You see, I have a kind of inborn abhorrence of Chaos. If it came again, if I thought it was

---

6 W. H. Auden, *New Year Letter* (London: Faber & Faber, copyright 1942), p. 40, used by permission of Random House, Inc.

here now—even a more subtle Chaos, a Chaos of the spirit, without the drowned cities and the careening stars—then I would simply leave the world to Chaos, I couldn't tolerate the world." [7]

Perhaps such a passage could only be written in our critical times, when dreams communicate reality. In any event, it brings us close to the meaning of the mythopoeic language of creation versus chaos.

A New Testament seer declares that in the end-time, when God's redemptive work is complete, the sea will be no more (Rev. 21:1), and there will be no more night (22:5). But the New Testament does not concentrate on that eschatological horizon. With the accents of good news it announces that already God in Christ has won the decisive victory over all the powers of evil, death, and darkness.

In Protestant circles there has perhaps been too great a tendency to say that the heart of the Christian message is Paul's great doctrine of "justification by faith," a doctrine which Paul Tillich once interpreted to mean: "I am accepted just as I am, even though I am unacceptable." Tillich's paraphrase is illuminating, and many will find it a helpful answer to Celia Copplestone's query to the psychiatrist in T. S. Eliot's play *The Cocktail Party:*

> It's not the feeling of anything I've ever *done,* which I might get away from, or of anything in me I could get rid of—but of emptiness, of failure towards someone, or something, outside of myself; and I feel I must . . . *atone*—is that the word? Can you treat a patient for such a state of mind? [8]

The Christian gospel does, indeed, minister to a person's state of inner chaos. But the weakness of an overemphasis upon justification by faith or its Tillichian paraphrase is that it is too individualistic, too psychological to do justice to the full

---

[7] Gladys Schmitt, *Confessors of the Name* (New York: Dial Press, 1952), p. 48. I am grateful to Professor Greer W. Boyce of Immanuel College, Victoria University, for calling my attention to this.

[8] T. S. Eliot, *The Complete Poems and Plays: 1909–1950* (New York: Harcourt, Brace & Co., 1958), p. 362. Used by permission of the publisher.

social and historical implications of the gospel of the New Testament. Paul's exposition of that theme occurs within the larger context of *Christus Victor:* the announcement that God in Christ is victorious over the principalities and the powers that hold dominion in this present age, and that this victory is a foretaste and anticipation of the final fulfillment:

> Then comes the end, when he [Christ] delivers the kingdom to God the Father after destroying every rule and every authority and power. For he must reign until he has put all his enemies under his feet. The last enemy to be destroyed is death.
>
> —I CORINTHIANS 15:24–26

Here the ancient theme of the conflict with the powers of chaos is pitched in a new key. The victory of the King is transposed out of the realm of mythology into the realm of history where men of faith celebrate the Event which emancipates them from all forms of bondage and enables them to walk in newness of life.

Carl Michalson, the successor to Edwin Lewis as teacher of systematic theology in the Theological School of Drew University, once preached a sermon on the great Resurrection chapter, I Corinthians 15, in which he developed the theme: the Christian gospel is a call to action in a conflict whose decisive Victory has already been won. His text was the last verse of that chapter: "Therefore, my beloved brethren, be steadfast, immovable, always abounding in the work of the Lord, knowing that in the Lord your labor is not in vain." This theologian's testimony rings true to the proclamation of the Christian faith. Yet it must be heard within the context of his incisive writings in which he attempted an exposition of what it means to say that Jesus Christ is the Event through which God calls the world to decision and inaugurates the eschatological age. In his posthumous book, *Worldly Theology,*[9] he observed that the *effect* of this Victory is to confer upon men the

---

[9] Carl Michalson, *Worldly Theology* [106]. See my summary of Michalson's theology in "The Power of the Interpreted Word," *The Christian Advocate,* June 16, 1966, pp. 7–8.

freedom which makes possible a new maturity. It is not only the freedom from all fears and cares of the world, but—even more important—the freedom which God gives his sons as heirs of his whole estate (see Gal. 4:1–7). Therefore, he ventured to say, Christians should not be zealous to convert men to Christ, i.e. to belief in his person; rather, their ambition should be to announce the dawn of the New Age and thereby to confirm and strengthen men in a responsible sonship which in some sense is theirs already.

The announcement that "in Christ God has turned the world over to men" is consistent with the biblical creation-faith as expressed in the Old Testament, especially in Genesis 1 and Psalm 8. Man is crowned with the supreme honor of being the agent who "subdues" the earth (Gen. 1:28), who exerts "dominion" over "all things" (Ps. 8:6). God has given man responsibility for the world. In a limited sense, he is intended to be a king who, in the ceaseless conflict of history, helps to sustain the creation in the fact of the menacing powers of chaos.

Selected Bibliography

No ATTEMPT HAS BEEN MADE to mention all works relevant to this subject; rather, the list includes selected books and articles which have proved especially helpful in the study, with special emphasis on works available in English. To facilitate footnote references, the items are listed by number. A few items which were added too late to go into the alphabetical sequence are listed at the end as "Addenda."

Reference Works
1. *The Oxford Annotated Bible with the Apocrypha*, ed. Herbert G. May and Bruce M. Metzger. New York: Oxford University Press, 1966.
2. *The Interpreter's Bible*, ed. G. A. Buttrick and others. New York: Abingdon Press, 1952–57.
3. *The Interpreter's Dictionary of the Bible*, ed. G. A. Buttrick and others. 4 vols. New York: Abingdon Press, 1962.
4. Charles, R. H., ed. *The Apocrypha and Pseudepigrapha of the Old Testament in English*. London: Oxford University Press, 1913; reprinted, 1963, 1964.
5. Pritchard, J. B., ed. *Ancient Near Eastern Texts Relating to the Old Testament*, 2nd ed. Princeton: Princeton University Press, 1955.
6. ———. *The Ancient Near East: An Anthology of Texts and Pictures*. Princeton: Princeton University Press, 1958.
7. Thomas, D. Winton, ed. *Documents from Old Testament Times*. New York: Harper Torchbook, 1961.

Other Books and Articles

8. Albright, William F. *Archaeology and the Religion of Israel*, 2nd ed. Baltimore: Johns Hopkins Press, 1946.

9. ————. *From the Stone Age to Christianity*, 2nd ed. New York: Doubleday & Co., 1957.

10. ————. "The Song of Deborah in the Light of Archaeology," *Bulletin of the American Schools of Oriental Research*, Vol. LXII (1936), pp. 26–31.

11. Anderson, Bernhard W. *Understanding the Old Testament*, 2nd ed. Englewood Cliffs, N. J.: Prentice-Hall, 1966.

12. ————. "The Earth is the Lord's: An Essay on the Biblical Doctrine of Creation," *Interpretation*, Vol. IX (1955), pp. 3–20.

13. ————. "Creation," in *The Interpreter's Dictionary of the Bible*. [3], Vol. I, pp. 725–32; "Water," *ibid.*, Vol. IV, pp. 806–10.

14. ————. "Exodus Typology in Second Isaiah," in *Israel's Prophetic Heritage*, ed. Bernhard W. Anderson and Walter J. Harrelson. New York: Harper & Row, 1962, pp. 177–95.

15. Barbour, Ian. *Issues in Science and Religion*. Englewood Cliffs, N. J.: Prentice-Hall, 1966. See also his earlier book, *Christianity and the Scientist*. New York: Association Press, 1960.

16. Barr, James. "Revelation through History in the Old Testament and in Modern Theology," *Interpretation*, Vol. XVII (1963), pp. 193–205.

17. ————. *Old and New in Interpretation: A Study of the Two Testaments*. New York: Harper & Row, 1966.

18. Barth, Karl. *Church Dogmatics*. Edinburgh: T. & T. Clark. III, 1 (1958); III, 3 (1961).

19. Bonhoeffer, Dietrich. *Creation and Fall: A Theological Interpretation of Genesis 1–3*. London: SCM Press, 1959.

20. Brandon, S. G. F. *Creation Legends of the Ancient Near East*. London: Hodder & Stoughton, 1963.

21. ————. "The Devil in Faith and History," *History Today*, July, 1963, pp. 468–78.

22. Bultmann, Rudolf. *Theology of the New Testament*, trans. Kendrick Grobel. Vols. I and II. New York: Charles Scribner's Sons, 1955.

23. ————. "New Testament and Mythology," in *Kerygma and Myth*, ed. H. W. Bartsch. New York: Harper Torchbook, 1961, pp. 1–44.

24. ————. "Ursprung und Sinn der Typologie als hermeneutischer Methode," *Theologische Literaturzeitung* 4/5 [1950], cols. 205–12.

25. Caird, G. B. *Principalities and Powers: A Study in Pauline Theology*. London: Oxford University Press, 1956.

26. Carus, Paul. *History of the Devil*. Chicago: Open Court, 1900.
27. Childs, Brevard. *Myth and Reality in the Old Testament*. London: SCM Press, 1960.
28. ———. "The Enemy from the North and the Chaos Tradition," *Journal of Biblical Literature*, Vol. 78 (1959), pp. 187–98.
29. Clements, R. E. *Prophecy and Covenant*. Studies in Biblical Theology, No. 43. London: SCM Press, 1965.
30. ———. *God and Temple*. Philadelphia: Fortress Press, 1965.
31. Cross, Frank M., Jr., and Freedman, David N. "A Royal Song of Thanksgiving: II Samuel 22 = Psalm 18," *Journal of Biblical Literature*, Vol. 72 (1953), pp. 15–34.
32. ———. "The Song of Miriam," *Journal of Near Eastern Studies*, Vol. XIV (1955), pp. 237–50.
33. Cross, Frank M., Jr. "Notes on a Canaanite Psalm in the Old Testament," *Bulletin of the American Schools of Oriental Research*, No. 117 (1950), pp. 19 ff.
34. ———. "Yahweh and the God of the Patriarchs," *Harvard Theological Review*, Vol. LV (1962), pp. 225–59.
35. ———. "The Divine Warrior in Israel's Early Cult," *Biblical Motifs*, ed. Alexander Altmann. Cambridge: Harvard University Press, 1966, pp. 11–30.
36. Dentan, R. C., ed. *The Idea of History in the Ancient Near East* (American Oriental Series, 38; New Haven, 1955).
37. Driver, G. R. "Mythical Monsters in the Old Testament," *Studi Orientalistici in onore di Giorgia Levi Della Vida*, Vol. I (Roma: 1956), pp. 234–49.
38. Eichrodt, Walther. *Theology of the Old Testament*, trans. J. A. Baker. Philadelphia: Westminster Press. I (1961); II (1967).
39. ———. "In the Beginning," in *Israel's Prophetic Heritage*, ed. Bernhard W. Anderson and Walter J. Harrelson. New York: Harper & Row, 1962, pp. 1–10.
40. ———. "Is Typological Exegesis an Appropriate Method?" in *Essays on Old Testament Hermeneutics*, ed. Claus Westermann; English trans. ed. James Luther Mays. Richmond: John Knox Press, 1963, pp. 224–45.
41. Eissfeldt, Otto. *Baal Zaphon, Zeus Kasios und der Durchzug der Israeliten durchs Meer*. Halle: Max Niemeyer Verlag, 1932.
42. ———. "Gott und das Meer in der Bible," *Studie Orientalia Ioanni Pedersen*. Copenhagen, 1953, pp. 76–84.
43. ———. "The Promises of Grace to David," in *Israel's Prophetic Heritage*, ed. Bernhard W. Anderson and Walter J. Harrelson. New York: Harper & Row, 1962, pp. 196–207.

44. Eliade, Mircea. *Cosmos and History: The Myth of the Eternal Return*, trans. Willard Trask. New York: Harper Torchbook, 1954.
45. ———. *The Sacred and the Profane*, trans. Willard Trask. New York: Harper Torchbook, 1961.
46. ———. *Myth and Reality*. New York: Harper & Row, 1963.
47. Engnell, Ivan. *Studies in Divine Kingship in the Ancient Near East*. Upsala: Almqvist and Wiksells, 1943.
48. Evans, Donald. *The Logic of Self-involvement*. London: SCM Press, 1963.
49. Finegan, Jack. *Light from the Ancient Past*, 2nd ed. Princeton: Princeton University Press, 1959.
50. Fisher, Loren R. "Creation at Ugarit and in the Old Testament," *Vetus Testamentum*, Vol. XV (1965), pp. 313–24.
51. Foerster, W. "Ktizo," *Theological Dictionary of the New Testament*, ed. G. Kittel; trans. G. Bromiley. Vol. III. Grand Rapids: Wm. B. Eerdmans, 1965, pp. 1000–1035.
52. Frankfort, H., and Frankfort, H. A., eds. *The Intellectual Adventure of Ancient Man*. Chicago: University of Chicago Press, 1946; republished in Pelican Books under the title *Before Philosophy* (1949).
53. Frankfort, Henri. *Kingship and the Gods: A Study of Ancient Near Eastern Religion as the Integration of Society and Nature*. Chicago: University of Chicago Press, 1948.
54. ———. *Ancient Egyptian Religion*. New York: Harper Torchbook, 1961.
55. Freedman, David Noel. See Nos. 31 and 32 in this bibliography.
56. Gaster, Theodor H. *Thespis: Ritual, Myth and Drama in the Ancient Near East*. New York: Harper Torchbook, 1966.
57. ———. *The Oldest Stories in the World*. Boston: Beacon Press, 1952.
58. ———. "Cosmogony," in *The Interpreter's Dictionary of the Bible*. [3], Vol. I, pp. 702–9.
59. ———. "Demon, Demonology," *ibid.*, Vol. I, pp. 817–24.
60. ———. "The Egyptian 'Story of Astarte' and the Ugaritic Poem of Baal," *Bibliotheca Orientalis*, Vol. IX (1952), pp. 82–85.
61. Gese, Helmut. "The Idea of History in the Ancient Near East and the Old Testament," in *Journal for Theology and Church*. New York: Harper & Row, 1965, Vol. I, pp. 49–64; trans. by James F. Ross from *Zeitschrift für Theologie und Kirche*, Vol. 55 (1958).
62. Gilkey, Langdon B. *Maker of Heaven and Earth: A Study of the Christian Doctrine of Creation*. New York: Doubleday & Co., 1959.

63. ———. "Cosmology, Ontology and the Travail of Biblical Language," *Journal of Religion*, Vol. 41 (1961), pp. 194–205.
64. Ginzberg, Louis. "Ugaritic Studies and the Bible," *Biblical Archaeologist*, Vol. VIII (1945), pp. 41–58.
65. Gordon, Cyrus H. "Leviathan: Symbol of Evil," in *Biblical Motifs*, ed. Alexander Altmann. Cambridge: Harvard University Press, 1966, pp. 1–9.
66. Gray, John. *The Legacy of Canaan*, 2nd ed. Leiden: Brill, 1965.
67. ———. "Canaanite Mythology and Hebrew Tradition," *Transactions of Glasgow University Oriental Society*, XIV (1953), pp. 47–57.
68. Gunkel, Hermann. *Schöpfung und Chaos in Urzeit und Endzeit*. Göttingen: Vandenhoeck und Ruprecht, 1895.
69. Guthrie, Harvey H., Jr. *Israel's Sacred Songs*. New York: Seabury Press, 1966.
70. Hamilton, Kenneth. "*Homo Religiosus* and Historical Faith," *Journal of Bible and Religion*, Vol. XXXIII (1965), pp. 211–22.
71. Harrelson, Walter. "Creation," *The Christian Scholar*, Vol. 39 (1956), pp. 45–49.
72. Hartshorne, M. H. *The Promise of Science and the Power of Faith*. Philadelphia: Westminster Press, 1958.
73. Heidel, Alexander. *The Babylonian Genesis: The Story of Creation*, 2nd ed. Chicago: University of Chicago Press, 1951.
74. Herberg, Will. "Beyond Time and Eternity: Reflections on Passover and Easter," *Christianity and Crisis*, Vol. IX, No. 6 (April 18, 1949), pp. 41–43.
75. ———. "Five Meanings of the Word 'Historical,'" *The Christian Scholar*, Vol. XLVII, No. 4 (1964), pp. 327–30.
76. Hividberg, Flemming. "The Canaanitic Background of Genesis I–III," *Vetus Testamentum*, Vol. X (1960), pp. 285–94.
77. Humbert, Paul. "Le problème du livre de Nahoum," *Revue d'Histoire et de Philosophie religieuses*, Vol. 12 (1932), pp. 1–15.
78. ———. "La relation de Genèse 1 et du Psaume 104 avec la liturgie du Nouvel-An israélite," *Opuscles d'un Hebraïsant*. Université de Neuchâtel, 1958, pp. 60–82.
79. ———. "Emploi et portée du verbe *bārā* [créer] dans l'Ancien Testament," *ibid.*, pp. 146–65.
80. ———. "*Qānā* en hébreu biblique," *ibid.*, pp. 166–74.
81. Jacob, Edmund. *Theology of the Old Testament*. New York: Harper & Bros., 1958.
82. Jacobsen, Thorkild. "Primitive Democracy in Ancient Mesopotamia," *Journal of Near Eastern Studies*, Vol. II (1943), pp. 159–72. See also Jacobsen's interpretation of Mesopotamian religion in No. 52. *Note:* Dr. Jacobsen plans to publish his lec-

tures on ancient Mesopotamian religion and thought under the title *Ancient Ways to Meaning*.

83. Johnson, Aubrey R. "Jonah 2.3–10: A Study in Cultic Phantasy," in *Studies in Old Testament Prophecy*, ed. H. H. Rowley. Edinburgh: T. & T. Clark, 1950, pp. 82–102.

84. ———. *The Vitality of the Individual in the Thought of Ancient Israel*. Cardiff: University of Wales Press, 1949.

85. ———. *Sacral Kingship in Ancient Israel*. Cardiff: University of Wales Press, 1955.

86. Kaiser, Otto. *Die mythische Bedeutung des Meeres in Aegypten, Ugarit und Israel*, zweite überarbeitete und in einem Nachtrag vermehrte Auflage. Berlin: Verlag Alfred Topplmann, 1959. See the full bibliography.

87. Kapelrud, Arvid S. *The Ras Shamra Discoveries and the Old Testament*. Oxford: Blackwell, 1962.

88. Knight, G. A. F. *A Christian Theology of the Old Testament*, 2nd ed. London: SCM Press, 1965.

89. Köhler, Ludwig. *Old Testament Theology*, 3rd ed., trans. A. S. Todd. Philadelphia: Westminster Press, 1953.

90. Kramer, Samuel Noah, ed. *Mythologies of the Ancient World*. New York: Doubleday & Co., 1961.

91. Kraus, Hans-Joachim. *Die Königsherrschaft Gottes im Alten Testament*. Tübingen: Mohr, 1951.

92. ———. *Psalmen*, Vols. I and II. *Biblischer Kommentar*. Neukirchen Verlag: 1960.

93. ———. *Worship in Israel*, trans. Geoffrey Buswell. Oxford: Blackwell, 1966.

94. Langton, Edward. *Essentials of Demonology*. London: Epworth Press, 1949.

95. ———. *Satan, a Portrait: A Study of the Character of Satan through all the Ages*. London: Skeffington & Son, 1945.

96. van der Leeuw, G. *Religion in Essence and Manifestation: A Study in Phenomenology*. New York: Harper Torchbook, 1963.

97. Lewis, Edwin. *The Creator and the Adversary*. New York: Abingdon-Cokesbury, 1948.

98. Lindeskog, G. "The Theology of Creation in the Old and New Testaments," in *The Root of the Vine*, ed. A. Fridrichsen. New York: Philosophical Library, 1953, pp. 1–22.

99. Ling, Trevor. *The Significance of Satan: New Testament Demonology and its Contemporary Relevance*. London: S.P.C.K., 1961.

100. May, Herbert G. "Some Cosmic Connotations of *Mayîm Rabbîm*, 'Many Waters,' " *Journal of Biblical Literature*, Vol. 74 (1955), pp. 9–21.

101. McKenzie, John L., S. J. "A Note on Psalm 73(74):13–15," *Theological Studies,* Vol. II (1950), pp. 275–82.

102. ———. "Myth and the Old Testament," in *Myths and Realities.* London: Geoffrey Chapman, Ltd., 1963, pp. 182–200.

103. Mendenhall, George E. *Law and Covenant in Israel and the Ancient Near East.* Pittsburgh: Biblical Colloquium, 1955.

104. ———. "Covenant," in *The Interpreter's Dictionary of the Bible.* [3], Vol. I, pp. 714–23.

105. Michalson, Carl. *The Rationality of Faith.* New York: Charles Scribner's Sons, 1963.

106. ———. *Worldly Theology: The Hermeneutical Focus of an Historical Faith.* New York: Charles Scribner's Sons, 1967.

107. Minear, Paul S. *Eyes of Faith: A Study in Biblical Point of View,* rev. ed. St. Louis: Bethany Press, 1960.

108. Mowinckel, Sigmund. *Psalmenstudien I–IV.* Kristiana: Dybwad, 1921–1924; reprinted Amsterdam: Verlag Schippers, 1961. See especially Vol. II: *Das Thronbesteigungsfest Jahwäs und der Ursprung der Eschatologie* (1922).

109. ———. *The Psalms in Israel's Worship,* Vols. I–II, trans. D. R. Ap-Thomas. New York: Abingdon Press, 1962.

110. ———. *He That Cometh,* trans. G. W. Anderson. New York: Abingdon Press, 1965.

111. ———. *The Two Sources of the Predeuteronomic Primeval History (JE) in Genesis 1–11.* Oslo, 1937. See also his exchange with W. F. Albright: "The Babylonian Matter in the Predeuteronomic Primeval History (JE) in Genesis 1–11," *Journal of Biblical Literature,* Vol. 58 (1959), pp. 87–103.

112. Muilenburg, James, *The Way of Israel.* New York: Harper & Row, 1961.

113. ———. "Isaiah, Chapters 40–66," in *The Interpreter's Bible.* [2], Vol. V, pp. 381–419.

114. ———. "A Liturgy on the Triumphs of Yahweh," in *Studia Biblica et Semitica, Theodoro Christiano Vriezen Dedicata.* Wageningen: H. Veenman & Zonen, 1966, pp. 233–51.

115. Napier, B. D. "On Creation Faith in the Old Testament," *Interpretation,* Vol. 16 (1962), pp. 21–42.

116. Newman, Murry L., Jr. *The People of the Covenant: A Study of Israel from Moses to the Monarchy.* New York: Abingdon Press, 1962.

117. Noth, Martin. *Ueberlieferungsgeschichte des Pentateuch.* Stuttgart: Kohlhammer Verlag, 1948); translation forthcoming by Bernhard W. Anderson and Alice F. Carse.

118. ———. "The 'Re-presentation' of the Old Testament in Proclamation," in *Essays on Old Testament Hermeneutics,* ed. Claus

Westermann; English trans. ed. by James Luther Mays. Richmond: John Knox Press, 1963, pp. 76–88.

119. ———. "God, King, People in the Old Testament," trans. Alice F. Carse, in *Journal for Theology and the Church,* Vol. I. New York: Harper Torchbook, 1965, pp. 20–48. Also in Martin Noth, *The Laws of the Pentateuch and Other Studies,* trans. D. R. Ap-Thomas. Philadelphia: Fortress Press, 1967, pp. 145–78.

120. Obermann, Julian. *Ugaritic Mythology: A Study of its Leading Motifs.* New Haven: Yale University Press, 1948.

121. Pannenberg, Wolfhart. "Redemptive Event and History," in *Essays on Old Testament Hermeneutics,* ed. Claus Westermann; English trans. ed. James Luther Mays. Richmond: John Knox Press, 1963, pp. 314–35.

122. Pedersen, Johannes. *Israel: Its Life and Culture,* I–II. London: Oxford University Press, 1926.

123. von Rad, Gerhard. *The Problem of the Hexateuch and Other Essays,* trans. E. W. Trueman Dicken. New York: McGraw-Hill Book Co., 1966, pp. 1–78.

124. ———. *Genesis,* trans. John Marks. Old Testament Library. Philadelphia: Westminster Press, 1961.

125. ———. *Deuteronomy,* trans. Dorothea Barton. Old Testament Library. Philadelphia: Westminster Press, 1966.

126. ———. *Old Testament Theology,* trans. D. M. G. Stalker. Vol. I (1962) and Vol. II (1965). New York: Harper & Row.

127. Renckens, Henricus, S. J. *Israel's Concept of the Beginning: The Theology of Genesis 1–3,* trans. Charles Napier. New York: Herder & Herder, 1964.

128. Rendtorff, R. "Die theologische Stellung des Schöpfungsglauben bei Deuterojesaja," *Zeitschrift für Theologie und Kirche,* Vol. LI (1954), pp. 3–14.

129. Reynold, P. *L'eau, sa vie et sa signification dans l'Ancient Testament,* 2nd rev. ed. Leiden; Brill, 1965.

130. Richardson, Alan. *Genesis I–XI.* Torch Commentary. London: SCM Press, 1953.

131. Ricoeur, Paul. "Culpabilité tragique et culpabilité biblique," *Revue d'Histoire et de Philosophie religieuses,* Vol. 33 (1953), pp. 285–307.

132. ———. *Finitude et culpabilité, II: La symbolique du mal.* Paris: Aubier, 1960; trans. Emerson Buchanan under the title, *The Symbolism of Evil.* New York: Harper Torchbook, 1967.

133. Ringgren, Helmer. *The Faith of the Psalmists.* London: SCM Press, 1963.

134. Rost, Leonhard. *Die Ueberlieferung von der Thronnachfolge*

Davids, Beiträge zur Wissenschaft vom Alten und Neuen Testament, 42. Stuttgart: Kohlhammer, 1926.

135. Rowley, H. H. "Zadok and Nehushtan," *Journal of Biblical Literature,* Vol. 58 (1939), pp. 113–32.

136. ————. "Melchizedek and Zadok (Genesis 14 and Psalm 110)," *Alfred Bertholet Festschrift.* Tübingen: J. C. B. Mohr, 1950, pp. 461–72.

137. Rozelaar, Marc. "The Song of the Sea," *Vetus Testamentum,* Vol. II (1952), pp. 221–28.

138. Russell, D. S. *The Method and Message of Jewish Apocalyptic* (200 B.C.–100 A.D.). The Old Testament Library. Philadelphia: Westminster Press, 1964.

139. Rylaarsdam, J. C. *Revelation in Jewish Wisdom Literature.* Chicago: University of Chicago Press, 1946.

140. Scott, R. B. Y. *Proverbs and Ecclesiastes.* The Anchor Bible. New York: Doubleday & Co., 1965.

141. ————. "Wisdom in Creation: the *'āmōn* of Proverbs viii 30," *Vetus Testamentum,* Vol. X (1960), pp. 213–23.

142. Speiser, E. A. *Genesis.* The Anchor Bible. New York: Doubleday & Co., 1964.

143. ————. "The Biblical Idea of History in its Common Near Eastern Setting," *Israel Exploration Journal,* Vol. VII (1957), pp. 201–16.

144. Steindorff, Georg, and Seele, Keith C. *When Egypt Ruled the East.* Phoenix Books. Chicago: University of Chicago Press, 1963.

145. Stuhlmueller, Carroll, C. P. "The Theology of Creation in Second Isaias," *Catholic Biblical Quarterly,* Vol. XXI (1959), pp. 429–67.

146. Terrien, Samuel. "Creation, Cultus, and Faith in the Psalter," *Horizons of Theological Education:* Essays in honor of Charles L. Taylor (*Theological Education,* Vol. II, No. 4 [1966], pp. 116–28).

147. ————. *The Psalms and Their Meaning for Today.* Indianapolis: Bobbs-Merrill Co., 1952.

148. Thielicke, Helmut. *How the World Began: Man in the First Chapters of the Bible,* trans. John W. Doberstein. London: James Clarke & Co., 1964.

149. de Vaux, Roland, O. P. *Ancient Israel.* 2 vols. New York: McGraw-Hill Book Co., 1965.

150. Vawter, Bruce, S. J. "Understanding Genesis," *Studies in Salvation History,* ed. C. Luke Salm, F. S. C. Englewood Cliffs, N. J.: Prentice-Hall, 1964, pp. 57–67.

151. Virolleaud, C. "Le Dieu de la mer dans la mythologie de Ras

Shamra," *Comptes-rendus de l'Académie des Inscriptions et Belles-Lettres* (1946), pp. 498–509.

152. Vriezen, Th. C. *An Outline of Old Testament Theology.* Holland: H. Veenman & Zonen, 1958.

153. Ward, James M. *Hosea: A Theological Commentary.* New York: Harper & Row, 1966.

154. Weiser, Artur. *The Psalms,* trans. Herbert Hartwell. Old Testament Library. Philadelphia: Westminster Press, 1962.

155. Wensinck, A. J. *The Ocean in the Literature of the Western Semites.* Verh. d. kon. Akad. v. Wetensch. te Amsterdam, Afd. Letterkunde, nieuwe reeks, deel XIX, No. 2, 1918.

156. Westermann, Claus. *A Thousand Years and a Day: Our Time in the Old Testament,* trans. Stanley Rudman. Philadelphia: Muhlenberg Press, 1962.

157. ———. *The Praise of God in the Psalms,* 2nd ed., trans. Keith R. Crim. Richmond: John Knox Press, 1961.

158. ———. *The Genesis Accounts of Creation,* trans. Norman E. Wagner. Facet Books. Philadelphia: Fortress Press, 1964.

159. ———. "God and His Creation," *Union Seminary Quarterly Review,* Vol. XVIII, No. 3 (March, 1963), pp. 197–209.

160. Wilder, Amos N. *Modern Poetry and the Christian Tradition: A Study of the Relation of Christianity to Culture.* New York: Charles Scribner's Sons, 1952.

161. ———. *Otherworldliness and the New Testament.* New York: Harper & Bros., 1954.

162. Wilson, John A. *The Burden of Egypt.* Chicago: University of Chicago Press, 1951.

163. Wright, G. Ernest. *Biblical Archaeology,* 2nd ed. Philadelphia: Westminster Press, 1962.

164. ———. "The Lawsuit of God," *Israel's Prophetic Heritage,* ed. Bernhard W. Anderson and Walter Harrelson. New York: Harper & Row, 1962, pp. 26–67.

165. ———. "The Temple in Palestine-Syria," *The Biblical Archaeologist Reader.* New York: Doubleday & Co., 1961, pp. 169–84.

166. ———. Article on "Schöpfung im AT," in *Die Religion in Geschichte und Gegenwart,* 3 Aufl. Tübingen: J. C. B. Mohr, 1961.

Addenda

167. Bultmann, Rudolf. "Faith in God the Creator," and "The Meaning of the Christian Faith in Creation," in *Existence and Faith,* ed. Schubert M. Ogden. New York: Meridian Books, 1960, pp. 171–82 and 206–25.

168. Galling, Kurt. "Der Charakter der Chaosschilderung in Gen.

1:2," *Zeitschrift für Theologie und Kirche,* Vol. 47 (1950), pp. 145–57.

169. Hermann, S. *"Die Naturlehre der Schöpfungsberichte," Theologische Literaturzeitung,* Vol. 86 (1961), cols. 413–24.

170. Konrad, J. F. *Abbild und Ziel der Schöpfung: Untersuchungen zur Exegese von Genesis 1 und 2 in Barth's Kirchlicher Dogmatik III.1.* Tübingen: J. C. B. Mohr, 1962.

171. Lambert, G. "La création dans la Bible," *Nouvelle Révue Théologique,* Vol. 75 (1953), pp. 252–81.

172. Ehrlich, Ernst W. *Die Kultsymbolik im Alten Testament und im nachbiblischen Judentum.* Stuttgart: Anton Hiersemann, 1959.

Index of Authors and Subjects

Index of Scriptural Passages